Zakir Magerramov

Cloud technologies

Zakir Magerramov

Cloud technologies

Lectures

ScienciaScripts

Imprint

Any brand names and product names mentioned in this book are subject to trademark, brand or patent protection and are trademarks or registered trademarks of their respective holders. The use of brand names, product names, common names, trade names, product descriptions etc. even without a particular marking in this work is in no way to be construed to mean that such names may be regarded as unrestricted in respect of trademark and brand protection legislation and could thus be used by anyone.

Cover image: www.ingimage.com

This book is a translation from the original published under ISBN 978-620-0-64385-8.

Publisher:
Sciencia Scripts
is a trademark of
Dodo Books Indian Ocean Ltd. and OmniScriptum S.R.L publishing group

120 High Road, East Finchley, London, N2 9ED, United Kingdom
Str. Armeneasca 28/1, office 1, Chisinau MD-2012, Republic of Moldova, Europe
Printed at: see last page
ISBN: 978-620-6-49987-9

Contents

History of the main types of high-performance computing

Probably back in 1975, it would have been fairly easy to count all the computers in the world. The first place we would have found them would have been in government offices, universities, and large corporations. A manufacturer like IBM would probably have given us a list of all the places where computers were installed. The power and speed of computers has increased every year. If we were to calculate a geometric growth rate and simply apply it to computer technology in 1975, we would be faced with an incredible increase in computing power. But of course, we all know that this is not what happens in reality.

The number of computers worldwide is also growing at an incredible rate. By some estimates, there are about one billion personal computers in use. But that's not the end of it. Computers in the form of embedded microprocessors can be found in telephones, tr3 players, car engines, electrical appliances and a host of other devices. Computers are everywhere.

In fact, it is conceivable that both the power and number of computers in the world are simultaneously growing exponentially, or at least at a similar rate. Obviously, this growth in the ability to manipulate information is beyond comprehension. Today, the computer revolution has turned its main force primarily on the information and communication spheres.

High performance computing is one of the most relevant and "hot" topics both in information technology and in many application areas.

The term "high-performance computing" (HPC) usually means not only performing large amounts of calculations, but also processing large amounts of data in a relatively short period of time.

As a rule, we can talk about high-performance computing when one or more of the following requirements are imposed on a hardware and software system:
-    high performance;
-    availability of a large amount of RAM;
-    the need to transfer large amounts of data;
-    the need to store and process large amounts of data.

High-performance computing is used, for example, in seismic exploration, on Internet services   , in   predicting
the spatial structure of proteins, etc.

Let's consider the example of Internet services. Everyone is well aware of such search services as Yandex, Google and others.

The way a search engine works is as follows. Special search robots - or spiders - visit all websites, "browsing" links and information on the pages. This information is processed in a special way - indexed - and stored in the database of the search engine. Later, when a user enters a query into a search box, the search engine transforms the query and searches its database for results.

The final result, which is presented on the Yandex page is taken from the database. The scheme would be very simple, if it weren't for one "but" - the scale of...

Below are some Internet facts that you should correlate with search engine performance:

- There are more than 900 million websites on the Internet. Potentially every search engine should index all of these sites.
- The number of Internet users in the world is 2.8 billion.
- There are about two terabytes of textual information in Runet (the Russian-language segment of the Internet) - Yandex should be guided by this information. In addition, there is also a search for pictures, videos, etc.
- There are about 1.6 billion unique images in Runet - these are photos and drawings, page design elements, banners, etc.
- As a result, every day Yandex processes more than 100 million requests. And the average response time should be within 300 milliseconds.

Thus, Internet services like search engines store and process huge amounts of information and also provide very high performance - these characteristics are specific to high-performance computing technologies.

In addition to search services, there are many other services on the Internet - also requiring the use of high-performance computing technologies for their successful operation.

In addition to the three examples presented above, there are many other fundamental and applied problems that require the involvement of high-performance computing technologies to solve effectively - all of these problems are grouped into the "Grand Challenges" group:

- weather and climate predictions;
- materials research;
- construction of semiconductor devices;
- development of pharmaceuticals;
- genetics;
- astronomy;
- transport tasks;
- hydro- and gas dynamics;
- controlled thermonuclear fusion;

- efficiency of combustion systems;
- geographic information systems;
- subsurface exploration;
- the science of the world's oceans;
- speech recognition and synthesis;
- image recognition.

So, there are tasks that can only be solved with high-performance computing. So what tools are available?

Here is a very simple classification of computers (see Figure 1.1). Mobile devices have the smallest computing power, but their number is huge. They are followed by personal computers (in terms of increasing performance and decreasing number), then servers. Finally, the pinnacle of computing devices is supercomputers.

The main characteristics of computing devices (computer) are performance. Now we will talk about the peak - i.e. theoretically maximum possible or upper limit - performance of a computing device (computer). As it happens, performance is calculated in the number of floating-point operations a computer can perform in one second (Floating Operations per Second - FLOPS, flops).

The peak performance of a modern personal computer is approximately up to 100 Gflops. Specialised servers have a performance between 100 and 500 Gflops.

High-performance computing - always parallel - is realised on devices commonly referred to as supercomputers.The   performance of the most powerful

of the world's supercomputers starts at 100 Tflops.

However, you should not try to use these numbers to categorise computing devices. Why?

Figure 1.1. Classification of computers

The Oxford Dictionary of Computer Science, published in 1986, states that *"a supercomputer is a very powerful computer with a performance of over 10 MFLOPS (millions of floating-point operations per second)"*. Today, this result is already overlapped not only by personal computers and mobile phones, but also by programmable calculators. In the early 90s, the supercomputer boundary was set around the 300 MFLOPS mark.

In 1996, specialists from the two leading "supercomputer" countries - the US and Japan - agreed to raise the supercomputer bar to 5 GFLOPS.

Now the supercomputer, which occupies the last place in the list of 500 most powerful supercomputers in the world has a performance of 415 Tflops.

As of June 2020, the leader of the ranking is the Japanese supercomputer Fugaku (415,530,000 GFLOPS)

As of June 2020, by the number of systems in the ranking, the countries are distributed as follows: China has 226 supercomputers (with 2 supercomputers out of the top 10 in terms of power installed in China). The USA has 114 machines in the Top 500 (with 4 supercomputers out of the Top 10 by power installed in the USA). Japan - 29 (with only one supercomputer in the Top 10, and at the same time the world's most powerful supercomputer Fugaku is installed in Japan), France - 19, Germany - 16, Holland - 15, Ireland - 14, Canada - 12, Great Britain - 10, Italy - 7, Singapore - 4, Brazil - 4, South Korea - 3, Saudi Arabia - 3, Norway - 3, Australia - 2, Russia - 2 (35 and 105 positions).

There are three main technologies for organising high-performance computing:

1. a computing cluster is a group of computers connected by high-speed

communication channels and representing a single hardware resource from the user's point of view;

2. A grid system is a group of geographically distributed computers connected by low-speed communication channels and representing a single hardware resource from the user's point of view;

3. "Cloud computing is the concept of providing ubiquitous and convenient on-demand network access to a common pool of customisable computing resources (e.g., data networks, processor and RAM resources, storage devices, applications and services - together and separately) that can be rapidly provisioned and released on demand with minimal operational costs.

Supercomputers are very expensive to build and maintain, so they are only available to leading scientific institutions and large companies. However, there is a need for high-performance computing in many organisations.

Therefore, it is   important to achieve high performance at a low cost

One solution to this problem is to create distributed computing systems.

Distributed computing is a rapidly developing field, which is associated with using the power of not only one personal computer, but also a large number of such devices. The essence lies in combining different computers with the help of special software. Thanks to this, a complex computational task can be divided into parts and distributed among hundreds or thousands of computers so that they can all work on its execution simultaneously. Distributed computing can take computing capabilities to an unprecedented level for solving complex problems in science and engineering.

One of the first and most famous cases of distributed computing application was recorded in the Human Genome Project. This international project started in 1990 and was completed in 2003. - two years ahead of schedule. The main goal of the project was to sequence the entire human DNA molecule and identify the approximately 25,000 individual genes that make up our genetic code. The process of decoding a DNA molecule and identifying each gene requires a huge amount of computing resources, and distributed computing played a significant role in this endeavour.

In recent years, the technology of "cell-by-cell" analysis has been rapidly developing, which makes it possible to study the level of gene activity not in a sample, but in each specific cell. With the help of this method it is possible to collect not 20000 data from one tissue sample, but 20000*N, where N is the number of cells, and not necessarily cancer cells. And we are talking about one more patient and one single tumour sample. And there are (potentially) millions and millions of such patients in the world, and each of them may have more than one tumour. This is how huge tables are born, endless rows of data).

The genetic information obtained from this project is stored in databases and is available to researchers and scientists on the internet. The result was a fantastic source of knowledge that is still being analysed by scientists and is guaranteed to lead to countless advances in the fields of genetics, bioengineering and medicine in the future.

Of particular interest in the field of distributed computing is the idea that the spare capacity of virtually every computer connected to the Internet network can be pooled and used to solve complex problems. Most computers, if left switched on, do nothing for long periods of time, especially at night. The idea of pooling them together for a kind of donation of free power is becoming popular in various fields.

A Stanford University project called Folding@home aims to solve a complex problem in a specialised area of biochemistry known as 'protein molecule folding'. Successful research in this area could help tackle cancer and diseases such as Huntington's or Parkinson's in the future. Another major user of this system is the Berkeley Open Software Platform for Distributed Computing (BOINC). This special software, developed at the University of California, Berkeley, allows participants to share their free computer power for a variety of scientific projects, including SETI ("Search for Extraterrestrial Intelligence"), Earth climate prediction, cancer research, astrophysics, and many others. You can download the programme to participate in these projects on the Internet.

In the future, we can assume that distributed computing will be of incredible importance. Moreover, they have already shaped the phenomenon that programmers call cloud computing. Essentially, it will lead to a new structure for harnessing the power of a huge number of computers as a necessary base: computing capabilities along with specialised applications will be distributed in a similar way to the way power plants distribute electricity. The trend towards the use of distributed and cloud computing offers incredible opportunities for the deployment of enormous new computing power in areas that will undoubtedly yield positive results in the development of fields such as science and medicine.

Grid systems

Another technology, which on the one hand has also influenced the emergence of the concept of cloud computing, but on the other hand has a number of significant differences. It is about collective or distributed computing (grid computing) - when a large resource-intensive computational task is distributed for execution among a set of computers united in a powerful computing cluster by the network in general or the Internet in particular.

When we switch on a fan or any electrical device, we care less about the source of power, where it comes from and how it is generated. The power source or electricity we get in our home is transmitted through a chain of networks that includes power plants, transformers, transmission lines and transmission stations. These components together make up the "power grid". Similarly, "Grid Computing" is the infrastructure that links computing resources such as PCs, servers, workstations and storage elements and provides the mechanism needed to access them (Figure 1.2).

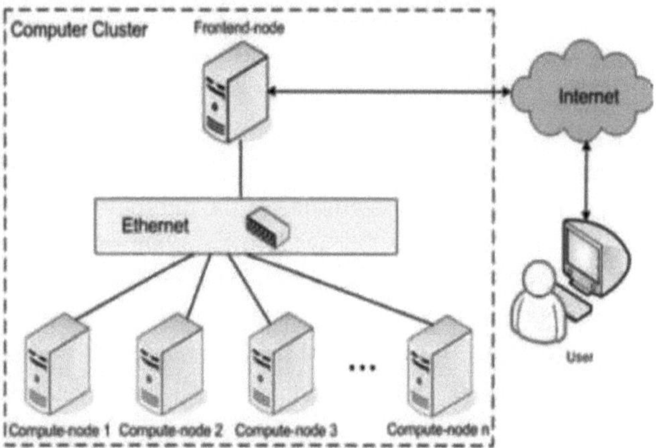

Fig. 1.2 Grid Computing

The establishment of a common protocol on the Internet has led directly to the rapid growth of online users. This has led to the need for more changes to current protocols and the creation of new ones. Currently, the Ipv4 protocol (the fourth version of the IP protocol) is widely used, but the limitation of the address space given by ipv4 will inevitably lead to the use of the ipv6 protocol. Over time, hardware and software improvements have been made, resulting in a common interface to the Internet. The use of web browsers has led to the use of the Cloud model, replacing the traditional information centre model.

In the early 1990s, Ian Foster and Karl Kesselman introduced the concept of Grid computing. They used the analogy of an electrical grid where users could connect and use a service. Grid computing relies heavily on techniques used in cluster computing models, where multiple independent groups act like a network simply because they are not all located within the same area.

Grid computing is a form of distributed computing in which a "virtual supercomputer" is represented as a cluster of networked, loosely coupled computers working together to perform a huge number of tasks.

In particular, the development of Grid-technologies made it possible to create so-called GRID-networks, in which a group of participants could jointly solve complex tasks. For example, IBM employees created an international grid-computing team, which enabled significant progress in the fight against the immune deficiency virus. Entire teams from different countries joined their computing power and helped to "calculate" and model the most promising forms for creating a cure for AIDS..."

Grid Computing is middleware for coordinating disparate IT resources on a network, allowing them to function as a single entity. This is more commonly used in scientific research and in universities for educational purposes. For example, a group of architecture students working on another project requires a special design tool and software for design purposes, but only a couple of them have accessed the design tool, the problem is how they can make the tool available to the rest of the students. To make available to other students they will place this design tool on the campus network, now the mesh will connect all these computers on the campus network and allow students to use the design tool required for their project from anywhere.

In practice, the boundaries between these (grid and cloud) types of computing are rather blurred. Today one can successfully meet "cloud" systems based on the distributed computing model, and vice versa.

The question of **how cloud computing and grid computing differ from each other is a subject of much** debate. However, as a rule, there is one thing that is generally agreed upon: cloud computing **grew out of the grid concept.**

Ian Foster defines the interaction of grid and cloud computing as follows:

"We believe that cloud computing doesn't just overlap with the concept of grid computing. In fact, clouds have grown out of grid computing and are based on the concept of grid infrastructure. The evolution of the approach is that instead of providing raw compute and storage resources, more abstract resources are provided in the form of services."

Cloud computing and grid computing are often confused, although their functions are almost the same, the approach to their functionality is different. Let's see how they work (Table 1.1).

Table 1.1. Cloud and grid computing functionalities

Cloud computing	Grid Computing
Cloud computing works more as a service provider for the use of computer resources	Grid computing uses available resources and interconnected computer systems to achieve a common goal
Cloud computing is. centralised model	Grid computing is A decentralised model where computations

	can be performed on many administrative models
A cloud is a collection of computers, usually owned by a single party	A grid is a set of computers that belong to multiple parties in different locations and are connected together so that users can share the aggregate power of resources
The cloud offers more services including all services such as web hosting, DB (database) support and more	The grid provides limited services
Cloud computing is usually provided within a single organisation (e.g. Amazon)	Grid computing combines resources located in different organisations

Cloud computing

IT-technologies appeared in our life not so long ago, but modern man at the moment cannot live without them. Now it is impossible to imagine how we would live without a phone, tablet or computer. But technology can not work forever. There are situations when it fails.

We store important files on our computers that we need for work, study and other activities. It is easy to imagine what happens to people when the operating system on a computer crashes and not all files can be recovered later. It should be borne in mind that an operating system lasts on average one to three years, and we are not always ready to lose the documents we need.

It is not always convenient to carry a flash card between work and home, and every day, constantly "flip" files back and forth, to carry a laptop or tablet computer - this is also not a convenient option, and after all, subconsciously want that these files would always be close at hand. Not always enough hard disc memory on your computer, and you need to save a file on your computer. And such a question arises: "What to delete, if everything is necessary?". In this case, "Cloud computing" comes to our aid. The idea behind cloud computing is this. You may not have any software on your computer, but only an Internet connection. Everything you need is on the Internet, and you can get what you need there. But whether it's free or paid - it depends on your needs.

However, the term "Cloud Computing" **is a** relatively recent phenomenon. According to the results of Google search engine analysis, the term "Cloud Computing" began to gain weight in late 2007 and early 2008, gradually replacing the phrase "Grid Computing". One of the first companies that gave the world this term was IBM, which in early 2008 launched the "Blue Cloud" project and sponsored the European project "Joint Research Initiative for Cloud Computing".

Cloud computing (from the English *cloud computing*, the term "cloud (dispersed) data processing" is also used) usually refers to the provision of computer resources and capacities to the user in the form of an Internet service. Thus, computing resources are provided to the user in a "pure" form, and the user may not know which computers are processing his requests, under which operating system it happens, etc.

Clouds are often compared to mainframes (mainframes), finding many similarities between them. The fundamental difference between the cloud and mainframes is that its computing power is theoretically unlimited. The second fundamental difference is that, simply put, mainframe terminals served only for interactive user interaction with the task being processed.

In the cloud, however, the terminal itself is a powerful computing device, capable of not only accumulating intermediate information, but also directly manage the global system of computing resources.

Among the earlier emerged (in the 1990s) data processing technologies, the so-called grid computing has gained some popularity. This direction was initially considered as an opportunity to use free resources of processors and to develop a system of voluntary lease of computing power. A number of projects (GIMPS, distributed.net, SETI@home) proved that this model of computing is quite effective. Today this technology is used to solve scientific and mathematical problems where significant computing resources are required. It is known that grid computing is also used for commercial purposes. For example, they are used to perform some labour-intensive tasks related to economic forecasting, seismic data analysis, development and study of properties of vaccines and new drugs. Indeed, grid computing and cloud computing share many similarities in architecture and applied principles. However, the cloud computing model is considered more promising today due to its much more flexible platform for working with remote computing resources.

Today, large-scale computing clouds consist of thousands of servers located in *data centres* (DCs). They provide resources for tens of thousands of applications that are simultaneously used by millions of users. Cloud technologies are a convenient tool for businesses that find it too expensive to maintain their own ERP, CRM or other servers that require additional hardware to be purchased and configured.

ERP (*Enterprise Resource* Planning) is an organisational strategy for integrating production and operations, labour management, financial management and asset management, focused on the continuous balancing and optimisation of enterprise resources through a specialised integrated suite of application software that provides a common data and process model for all areas of the enterprise.

CRM (Customer Relationship Management) is a customer relationship management system, i.e. application software designed to automate customer (client) relationship strategies, in particular to increase sales, optimise marketing and improve customer service by storing customer information and relationship history, establishing and improving business procedures and then analysing the results.

Cloud services such as those provided by Google ("Documents", "Calendar", etc.) are gradually becoming widespread among private users due to their convenience.

The reasons for the increasing popularity of cloud technologies are clear: the applications are very diverse and save on maintenance, staff and infrastructure. Hardware can be greatly simplified when processing data and storing information in remote data centres. All these problems are almost entirely shifted to the service provider.

In addition, this approach allows software to be standardised even if different operating systems (Windows, Linux, MacOS, etc.) are installed on the company's computers. Cloud technologies facilitate access to company data for both clients and employees who are away from the office but can connect via the Internet.

It is clear that using cloud computing is much more convenient. The most important disadvantage, which can be immediately noticed, is the complete dependence on the provider of these services. In fact, the enterprise (user) is held hostage to the service provider and the Internet access provider. Although the reliability of cloud computing providers is increasing, a lot of effort is needed to ensure data reliability and security, such as having redundant communication channels, redundant capacity to be able to switch to them and, of course, to think about information availability and security. In addition, cloud computing is completely unsuitable for businesses dealing with state and military secrets. No commission will issue a certificate for such a system when working with non-public information.

Modern cloud technologies are not only used in off-the-shelf network and server equipment, but are also gradually penetrating the embedded cloud market and causing a major restructuring of the market. The introduction of embedded systems leads to the placement of computer processors in such products as resource consumption meters, smart sensors, M2M modules, cars, household appliances, etc. This makes it possible to control the operation of devices, collect data and provide interactive features by connecting to a computer network.

The idea of connecting all sorts of devices to a global network is called the Internet of Things (IoT). According to Kevin Dallas, general manager of Microsoft Windows Embedded, the idea of the Internet of Things has been around for many years, but it has lacked one link to build such a network - the cloud.

As the number of embedded computers increases due to falling processor prices and the ubiquity of the Internet, the amount of data being transferred and processed (often in real time) is also increasing. It can therefore be assumed that the role of the Internet of Things and cloud computing will increase in the coming years.

History of the emergence of cloud technology

The first idea of what we today call cloud computing was voiced by **Joseph Carl Robnett Licklider** (1915 - 1990, known in the scientific and IT environment as J.C.R. or "Lick") in 1970. During these years he was responsible for the creation of the ARPANET. His idea was that *every person on earth would be connected to a network from which they would receive not only data but also programmes*.

In the same period, another scientist **John McCarthy** (1927-2011) suggested that *computing power would be provided to users as a service*.

At this point, the development of cloud technology was halted until the 90s, after which a number of factors contributed to its development.

The expansion of Internet bandwidth, in the 90's did not allow for a significant leap in development in cloud technology, as virtually no company or technology of the time was ready for it. However, the very fact of Internet acceleration gave a boost to the rapid development of cloud computing.

One of the most significant developments in this area was the emergence of Salesforce.com in 1999. This company was the first to provide access to its application through a website, in fact, this company was the first company to provide its software as a service.

The next step was the development of a cloud-based web service by Amazon in 2002. This service allowed to store, store information and perform calculations.

In 2006, Amazon launched a service called Elastic Compute cloud (EC2) as a web-based service that allowed its users to run their own applications. Amazon EC2 and Amazon S3 services were the first cloud computing services available, and are still considered one of the leaders in cloud computing.

Another milestone in the development of cloud computing came when Google created, Google Apps platform for web applications in the business sector.

In 2008, Microsoft announced its plans in this area. And Microsoft announced not just a service, but a full-fledged cloud operating system Windows Azure.

A significant role in the development of cloud technologies has been played by virtualisation technologies, in particular, software that allows the creation of virtual infrastructure (for example, VMware Corporation's project VMware vCloud).

The development of hardware has contributed not so much to the rapid growth of cloud technologies as to the availability of this technology for small businesses and individuals. As for technical progress, a significant role in this was played by the creation of multi-core processors and increasing the capacity of information storage devices (the emergence of a set of free software projects with open source code - OpenStack).

In July 2008, HP, Intel, and Altaba (formerly Yahoo) announced the creation of a global, multi-site, open source Cloud Computing Test Bed to advance research and development in cloud computing.

The launch of Google Apps in 2009 is noted as the next important step in the popularisation and understanding of cloud computing. Between 2009 and 2011, several important generalisations of cloud computing concepts were formulated, such as proposing a model of private cloud computing relevant for use within organisations, highlighting different service models (SaaS, PaaS, IaaS). In 2011, the National Institute of Standards and Technology formed a definition that structured and fixed all the interpretations and variations of cloud computing in a single concept.

Thus, from history, we can understand that the basis for the creation and rapid development of cloud technology was based on large Internet services such as Google, Amazon, and technological progress, which, in fact, suggests that the emergence of cloud computing was only a matter of time.

The term "cloud technology" itself only became established in 2007. However, until now there is no universal definition, because in the process of development the wording is subject to new and new changes. At the same time, cloud technologies are understood as the provision of computer resources and capacities to the user in the form of Internet services.

Thus, it can be considered that **grid and cloud computing complement each other**. Grid computing brings together heterogeneous computing resources into a single computing environment, providing the starting point and foundation for cloud computing. Cloud computing provides a higher level of abstraction by providing computing resources to end users (whether private clients or organisations) in the form of services.

However, the future of cloud computing is still much larger than distributed systems, and not every cloud service requires large computing power with a single management infrastructure or centralised payment processing point.

Key factors in the development of cloud technologies

Key factors in the development of cloud technologies

The term "Cloud" comes from a network design that was used by network engineers to represent the location of various network devices and their interconnectivity. The shape of this network was looks like a cloud (Figure 2.1).

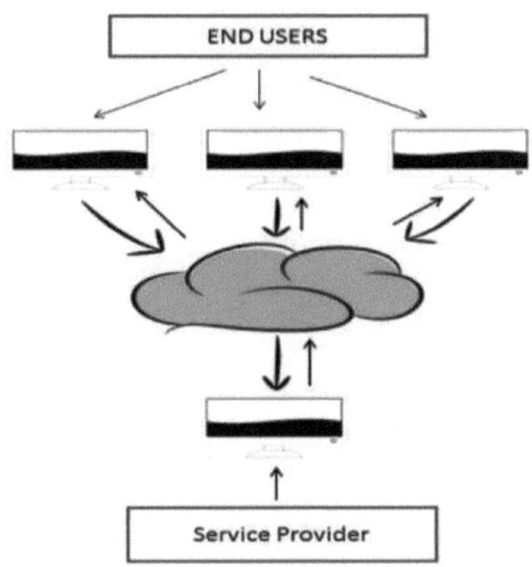

Figure 2.1. Network design, from the network design from which the term "Cloud" originated

Among the earlier emerged (in the 1990s) data processing technologies, the so-called **grid computing has** gained some popularity. **This direction was initially considered as an opportunity to use free resources of processors and to develop a system of voluntary lease of computing power. A number of projects (GIMPS, distributed.net, SETI@home) proved that this model of computing is quite effective. This technology is used to solve scientific and mathematical problems where significant computing resources are required. It is known that grid computing is also used for commercial purposes. For example, they are used to perform some labour-intensive tasks related to economic forecasting, seismic data analysis, development and study of properties of vaccines and new drugs. Indeed, grid computing and cloud computing share many similarities in architecture and applied principles. However, the cloud computing model is considered more promising today due to its much more flexible platform for working with remote computing resources.**

Today, large-scale computing clouds consist of thousands of servers located in *data centres* (DCs). They provide resources for tens of thousands of applications that are simultaneously used by millions of users.

Definition of cloud computing:

Ian Foster: "Cloud computing is a large-scale distributed computing paradigm based on economies of scale in which a pool of abstracted, virtualised, dynamically scalable computing resources, storage resources, platforms and services are made available on demand to external users over the Internet."

Berkeley Lab: "Cloud computing is not just about applications delivered as services over the Internet, but also about the hardware and software systems in data centres that deliver those services...".

Luis Vacuero (Research Engineer IV, Hewlett-Packard Labs), 2008: *"The* **cloud** is a large pool of readily usable and readily available virtualised resources (such as hardware, services, etc.). These resources can be dynamically reallocated (scaled) to adjust to dynamically changing workloads, ensuring optimal resource utilisation. This pool of resources is usually provided on a pay-as-you-use basis. The cloud owner guarantees the quality of service based on certain agreements with the user".

US National Institute of Standards and Technology (NIST), 2011: **Cloud computing** is an information technology concept that involves providing ubiquitous and convenient on-demand networked access to a common pool of configurable computing resources (e.g., data networks, servers, storage devices, applications, and services, either together or separately) that can be rapidly provisioned and released with minimal operational costs or calls to the provider.

The foundation for cloud infrastructure is data storage. For this purpose, both unstructured storage (i.e., distributed file systems) and databases with different degrees of structuring are used. The main obstacle in building distributed storage is formulated in the form of the so-called CAP theorem:

Theorem (Brewer, 2002). There does not exist a distributed computer system satisfying three conditions simultaneously:

• Consistency - the system looks like a whole to an outside observer, so that the state of the system for different nodes cannot be inconsistent (but nodes can "lag");

• Availability - Each data request will receive a response in a finite amount of time about the success of its fulfilment;

• Scalability (Partition tolerance) - the system continues to function despite possible loss of messages between nodes or failure of a part of the system.

"The cloud is not a place, but a way of managing IT resources, replacing local machines and private data centres with virtual infrastructure. In the cloud, users have access to virtualised computing, networking and storage resources provided online by a remote provider. Resources are allocated instantly on demand, which is useful when you need to rapidly expand or shrink your infrastructure to meet changing demand.

<u>Cloud computing</u> is a technology that allows data to be stored and processed remotely in the cloud. Data processing centres (DPCs) are used for this purpose. A company using cloud computing does not have to build its own IT infrastructure - everything it needs can be provided by a provider. All you need is access to the internet to open a website or application.

With the increasing number of computer and mobile device users, data storage has become a priority in all fields. Large and small businesses today thrive on their data, and they have spent huge amounts of money to maintain that data. A strong IT support and storage centre is required. Not all companies can afford the high cost of internal IT infrastructure and backup services. For them, Cloud Computing is a cheaper solution. Perhaps its efficiency in data storage, computing and lower maintenance costs has attracted larger companies.

Cloud computing reduces the need for hardware and software on the user side. The only thing a user needs to be able to run is the interface software of cloud computing systems, which can be as simple as a web browser, and the cloud network takes care of the rest. We have all experienced cloud computing at some point of time, some of the popular cloud services that we have used or are still using are email services like gmail, hotmail or yahoo etc.

Cloud computing (from the English *cloud computing*, the term "cloud (dispersed) data processing" is also used) usually refers to the **provision of computer resources and capacities to the user in the form of an Internet service**. Thus, computing resources are provided to the user in a "pure" form, and the user may not know which computers are processing his requests, under which operating system it happens, etc.

We already know what cloud computing is. Let's look at its advantages and disadvantages.

Advantages and disadvantages of cloud technologies

Like any technology, cloud technology has both advantages and disadvantages. The **main advantages include**:

1. Accessibility - clouds are accessible to everyone, from anywhere there is internet, from any computer with a browser.

2. Flexibility - unlimited computing resources (memory, CPU, disks)

3. Lower IT infrastructure and computer costs for users

4. Reliability - the reliability of "clouds", especially those located in specially equipped data centres, is very high, as such data centres have redundant power supplies, security, professional staff, regular data backup, high Internet bandwidth, high resistance to DDOS attacks.

5. Ease of use - no special skills are required to use cloud services, just choose a cloud provider and you're good to go

6. Improved performance

7. Fewer maintenance problems

8. Instant software updates

9. Improved compatibility between operating systems

10. Backup and restore

11. Performance and scalability - the user has the ability to increase or decrease the amount of resources used at any time as needed.

12. Increased capacity

13. Mobility - the user is not tied to a single workplace, as he can access cloud services from anywhere in the world if he has an internet connection.

14. Security - through the use of virtualisation, state-of-the-art security systems and constant supervision by professionals, a high level of security

and safety of customer data in the cloud is guaranteed, but if negligent, the effect can be the complete opposite

15. More computing power - you as a cloud user can use all of the cloud system's computing power, paying only for actual usage time.

16. Highly technologically advanced - users have access to a huge pool of computing power, allowing them to work much more efficiently.

For all its advantages, cloud technology has **some serious drawbacks:**

1. Persistent network connection - accessing cloud services requires a persistent Internet connection

2. Software and customisation - there are limitations on the software that can be deployed on clouds and made available to the user. The software user has limitations in the software that can be used and sometimes does not have the ability to customise it for their own purposes

3. Confidentiality - the confidentiality of data stored on public clouds is currently a matter of much debate, but in most cases experts agree that you should not store the most valuable documents for the company on the public cloud, as there is no technology that would guarantee 100% confidentiality of the data stored

4. Reliability - as far as reliability of information storage is concerned, it's safe to say that if you lose information stored in the cloud, you've lost it forever

5. Security - the cloud itself is a fairly secure system, but if it is infiltrated, an intruder has access to a huge data storage. Another disadvantage is the use of virtualisation systems that use the kernels of standard operating systems such as Linux, Windows, etc. as a hypervisor, which allows viruses to be used

6. Delay in data transmission between the client and the data centre. Data is transmitted from the client to the data centre and back, traversing many kilometres of networks. This can create delays.

7. Complex and expensive infrastructure. If a company doesn't want to use a public cloud, it opts for a private or hybrid cloud. But setting up and maintaining a large data centre in production is a costly task

8. Expensive hardware - to build its own cloud, a company needs to allocate significant material resources, which is not favourable to newly established and small companies.

The main difference between a cloud-based software solution and a regular one is that all the information you work with will be stored not on your hard drive, but on a remote server.

One of the significant features of the "cloud" model of software platforms is that there is no need to scrutinise system requirements, buy more and more expensive components and multi-stage programme installation: you just need to open a browser, go to a certain website and create an account there, following the rules of the service. Once you have done this, you can use your profile from any device (personal computer, laptop, PDA, tablet or smartphone) without worrying about transferring information from one medium to another: after all, it is stored on the server, for access to which you only need an Internet connection, login and password.

Features of cloud computing

The features of cloud computing are shown in Figure 2.2.

On the owner side of computing resources, cloud computing is focused on providing information resources to external users.

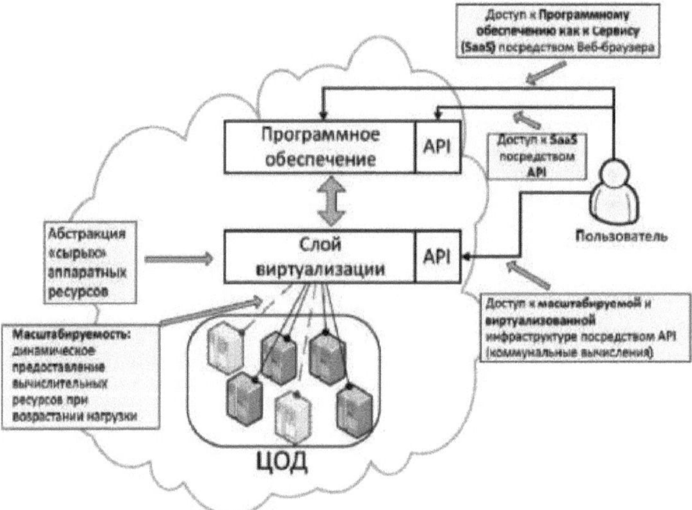

Fig 2.2. Features of cloud computing

On the user side, cloud computing is the receipt of information resources in the form of a service from an external provider, for which payment is made depending on the amount of resources consumed according to a set tariff. The key characteristics of cloud computing are *scalability* and *virtualisation*.

Scalability is the ability to dynamically adjust information resources to changing workloads, such as an increase or decrease in the number of users, changes in the required storage capacity or computing power.

Virtualisation is mainly used to provide *abstraction* and *encapsulation*. *Abstraction* allows us to unify the "raw" computing, communication resources and information storage in the form of a pool of resources and

22

build a unified resource layer that contains the same resources but in an abstracted form. These are presented to users and upper layers of cloud systems as virtualised servers, server clusters, file systems and DBMSs.

Application *encapsulation* enhances security, manageability and isolation. Another important feature of cloud platforms is the ***integration of*** hardware resources and system software with applications that are delivered to the end user as services.

Obligatory characteristics of cloud computing

> ***On-demand self-service - the*** consumer independently determines and modifies computing needs such as server time, access and processing speeds, and the amount of data stored without interacting with a service provider representative;

> ***Universal network access*** - services are available to consumers over the data network regardless of the terminal device used;

> ***Resource pooling - A*** service provider pools resources to serve a large number of customers into a single *pool* to dynamically reallocate capacity between customers in the face of constantly changing capacity demand;

> ***Elasticity*** - services can be provided, expanded, contracted at any point in time, without additional costs of interaction with the supplier, usually in an automatic mode;

> ***Consumption accounting - the*** service provider automatically calculates the consumed resources at a certain level of abstraction (e.g. storage capacity, bandwidth, number of users, number of transactions), and based on this data estimates the amount of services provided to consumers.

There is a perception that Edge and Fog computing will eventually replace cloud solutions that have become commonplace. But this is not the case at all. Yes, there are times when edge technologies offer greater benefits than fully centralised cloud platforms, especially from a storage perspective. But it's always the hybrid and multi-cloud concept that remains at the core of enterprise IT infrastructure. In other words, edge and fog computing will not replace cloud computing, because it is, in fact, nothing more than an "extension" and "extension" of the cloud.

Cloud systems use specific computation methods to process data. One of the most common models of such computation is **MapReduce**, proposed by Google. In its essence, it resembles the use of *map* and *reduce functions* in functional programming languages (for example, these functions are available in Python), only for distributed systems. Among the algorithms used to process cloud data are machine learning (e.g., for contextual advertising or face recognition in photos) and indexing (e.g., for full-text search of large arrays of documents).

Cloud computing use case study - Royal Mail

Royal mail group, the postal service in the UK, is the only publicly owned organisation in the UK, serving more than 24 million customers through its 12,000 post offices and 3,000 individual processing points. Its logistics systems and parcel service worldwide handle around 404 million parcels a year. And to do so, they need an efficient communication environment. They realised the advantage of cloud computing and implemented it in their system. It has shown outstanding performance in cross-community communication.

Before moving to the cloud, the organisation was struggling with outdated software, which was causing a drop in efficiency. Once the organisation moved to a cloud-based system, 28,000 employees received a new collaboration suite, giving them access to tools such as instant messaging and presence reporting. Employees got more storage space than on a local server. Employees became much more productive.

Royal Mail Group's second strategic move was to migrate from physical servers to virtual servers, up to 400 servers, to create a private cloud based on Microsoft Hyper V, to give a fresh perspective and extra desktop space to its employees, as well as providing the latest modern sharing environment.

The HyperV project from RMG (Royal Mail Group) is expected to save them around £1.8m in the future and improve the efficiency of the organisation's internal IT system.

Scope of cloud computing

Cloud technologies are used everywhere: in the public sector, manufacturing, retail, IT companies, financial services and telecommunications. It is hard to imagine modern life without email, Google Docs, app shops and public clouds like Dropbox, Google Drive or Yandex. Disk.

"Cloud Computing has been developing most dynamically over the last decade, with technology penetration rates in developed countries exceeding 90%. Cloud and data centre operators have considerable expertise in this area and can provide users with the most advanced technological solutions in the field of on-demand IT infrastructure".

Along with cloud computing, there are fog computing and edge computing. Let's understand the differences between these types of computing, their advantages and disadvantages, and in which industries they are most relevant.

Fog computing (Fog computing)

Fog computing is a technology whereby data storage and processing takes place in a local network between the end device and the data centre. "Fog", unlike "cloud", is closer to the users. It is a decentralised system that filters information coming into the data centre.

The benefits of fog computing:

• Cloud load relief. Using fog technologies along with cloud technologies helps in reducing the load on the data centre. Local servers process data and send only the most important data to the data centre.

• Real-time data transmission. "Fog" is closer to the user, so the time to process and transfer information is reduced.

• Additional security. You can set up another layer of security on the local network - virtual firewall, traffic segmentation, or something else.

The disadvantages of fog computing:

• Problems with network nodes. Decentralised networks are less reliable than large data centre networks.

Scope of application of fog computing

Fog computing is used to communicate Internet of Things (IoT) devices. With fog, data is transmitted and analysed with almost no latency, which is critical for some IoT devices, such as sensors in unmanned vehicles.

"Simply put, fog computing is customised for machine-to-machine communication and can be applied in any industry where it is used - manufacturing, healthcare, energy, finance and others."

Edge computing

Edge computing is a technology for processing and storing data on an endpoint device. They are even closer to the user than cloud and fog.

Advantages of boundary calculations:

• Virtually zero latency in data transmission. Computations are performed on endpoint devices, so information does not need to traverse kilometres of networks to reach the data centre.

• Reliable computing. Data is processed even when there is no internet connection.

• Security. All information stays on your device. You don't have to transfer it to the public cloud.

Disadvantages of boundary calculations:

• Costs for equipment and employees. The user of the technology will have to buy and configure equipment and engage specialists. This is more complicated than connecting to a public cloud.

Scope of application of boundary calculations

The application areas of boundary and fog technologies overlap in many ways. Their main advantage is the speed of data transmission and analysis. Therefore, these technologies are used where real-time information processing is important - for example, in the areas of IoT and VR/AR (VR - Virtual Reality, AR - Augmented Reality).

In manufacturing, edge computing is needed for timely equipment maintenance, in the oil industry it can help detect faults and leaks, and in banking, the technology can help make quick decisions on loans or detect fraud. In all of these examples, edge computing helps you to act without delay.

"Edge has found widespread use in industrial enterprises. Cloud computing demonstrates flexibility and efficiency, but the proliferation of IoT and mobile computing has led to a limited frequency range for processing. Also nuanced is the fact that smart equipment in enterprises does not always require cloud connectivity to perform calculations. In such cases, network designers are relying on the edge to improve processing efficiency."

Cloud technologies have penetrated all spheres of our lives - both personal and professional. Let's take a closer look at their application.

In the educational process

Cloud computing is a set of resources that can be shared anywhere, regardless of the location of the users. Thanks to the introduction of such technologies, it has become possible to unite teachers and students on a single educational platform. It is in the cloud that distance learning takes place in schools, universities, and courses.

From a student perspective, access to cloud infrastructure allows students to modernise their approach to education. The software allows teachers to share notes and lesson plans, and students to do away with heavy textbooks and outlining.

The applications have minimal hardware requirements - this is important for accessible education. You can learn from a computer, laptop, tablet or phone.

In medicine

According to a West Monroe Partner report, 35 percent of healthcare organisations surveyed store more than 50 percent of their data or infrastructure in the cloud. Healthcare providers are using the cloud to improve efficiency, streamline workflows, reduce costs associated with care delivery, and provide personalisation in patient care and treatment.

Cloud technology allows access to patient data collected from multiple sources, sharing information with stakeholders. All of this helps to make diagnoses and prescribe treatment faster. In complex cases, it is possible to quickly create a medical consensus or provide a virtual presence of a doctor.

Applying Data Science techniques and artificial intelligence algorithms to cloud-based patient data can accelerate medical research. Thanks to advanced computing capabilities, the processing of large amounts of data is becoming realistic and accessible even for hospitals in third world countries.

In banking

Enhanced cloud security controls make it easier to perform everyday tasks in banking.

The banking and finance sector requires large amounts of data to be processed on a daily basis - it's more convenient and cheaper to do it in the cloud. This is how banks can turn large initial capital expenditures into smaller ongoing capital expenditures. In addition to high levels of data protection, fault tolerance, business continuity, automatic backups, financial organisations can quickly develop, test and deploy new products.

Cloud computing allows non-critical services, including software patches, maintenance and other issues, to be moved to the cloud. As a result, banks can focus on financial services rather than IT.

In commerce

The cloud platform is ideal for trading. It is available, scalable to store huge amounts of market data, perform various analyses (e.g. risk analysis). To accelerate market entry, traders require a wide range of applications and services and high-performance computing solutions.

Cloud technology in retail provides real-time access to all operational and financial data. The entire lifecycle of processes is optimised: merchandising, marketing, purchasing, sales, feedback. You can collect customer information, analyse it, and develop advertising campaigns.

In business

Cloud technology opens up opportunities to improve the efficiency of all business processes. As a company grows, computing power can be quickly scaled up or shut down if the need goes away. This frees up budget for other development opportunities.

Employees of companies can access information that will allow them to serve customers at any time of day and from anywhere in the world. At the same time, employees can perform their duties from the office or from home - virtual desktops are used to access files from anywhere, and employee productivity can be monitored in real time.

In the economy

Cloud technologies are helping to grow both local and global economies. They have enormous potential to drive economic transformation, providing growth for individual companies and the public sector with minimal investment. Their effective implementation creates a level playing field for businesses of all sizes, equalising start-ups and large corporations, creating a competitive environment, which has a positive impact on the economy as a whole.

A study by the Boston Consulting Group found that revenue for businesses that have embraced cloud technology increased by

15% faster than those who worked solely on their own hardware and computing power. What did it do in terms of the economy? Fast-growing businesses created new jobs, which provided social and economic benefits to the economy in the region.

In logistics

Cloud computing has found widespread use with logistics service providers. Because of the nature of logistics, where there is a need for a large number of stakeholders to interact effectively, the cloud is the place where everything can be connected without great expense.

Supply chain transactions take place between multiple stakeholders, characterised by complexities associated with the disconnect between data, processes and people. Cloud-based logistics technology addresses these challenges. The result is a more predictable supply chain. Companies around the world are moving away from outdated technology, manual processes and moving to software in the cloud to predict and solve problems before they occur.

A constant flow of data allows you to find the most favourable offer among service providers (e.g. the company with the lowest freight price), and real-time monitoring will make it possible to merge multiple logistics flows to eliminate downtime.

In the industry.

Cloud services have traditionally been designed horizontally, but the current trend is towards vertical programmes that are designed specifically for specific industries.

For example, the automotive industry uses a unified cloud environment to share data between suppliers and parts manufacturers. In addition, the growing popularity of unmanned vehicles is helping major market players interpret a large amount of data to develop this trend.

In management

By providing mobility for employees, scalability and speed of deployment for organisations, cloud computing is changing the way businesses are run.

Managers can track employee performance and create fair motivation systems. Cloud technologies help to analyse the current state of affairs in the company and plan effective development strategies based on data received from various sources.

Comparison of Fog vs Cloud Computing (Fog vs Cloud)

The rise of smartphones and their applications are enabling users to access more and more data, processing power, and giving them the ability to control end devices in real time.

However, the traditional centralised Cloud Cloud architecture and the limited bandwidth of Core layer networks prevents large amounts of data from end sensors and sensors from being sent there for computation and analysis.

Fog Computing, on the other hand, enables Fog node devices at the edge of the network to perform some data processing at the point where the data is received and used, in order to reduce the latency of the exchange and the amount of data sent to the Cloud, as well as to perform local analytics (see Figure 2.3).

The average lifetime of a server in cloud data centres is about two years. For business applications that generate large amounts of data, such frequent hardware upgrades are not only technically difficult, but also very expensive. Instead of investing, organisations' IT departments have to spend all their time keeping their IT system up to date with current business requirements. However, at the edge of the network in small distributed data centres, server infrastructure components can last up to eight years. Research shows that solutions based on centralised Cloud alone are much more costly than those based on a hybrid Cloud+Fog architecture.

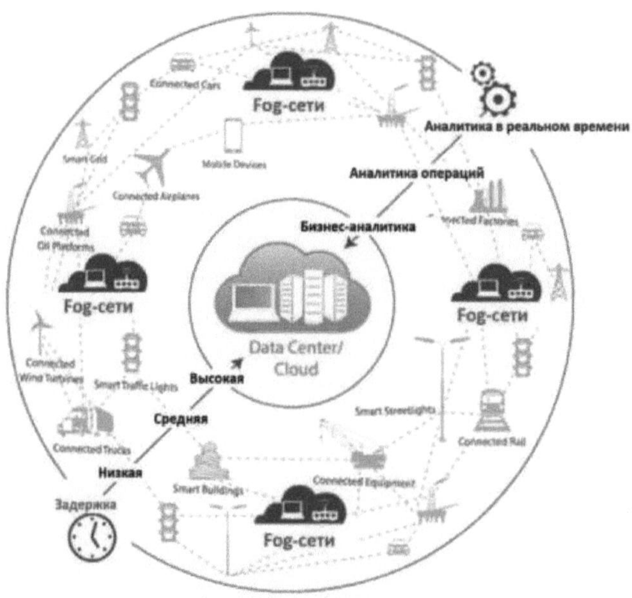

 Delayed data exchange and analytics operations in Fog network (source: Dataconomy 2016).

Another issue related to Cloud is computation speed and communication latency. When transferring to the cloud, the computation speed decreases and the communication latency increases. However, data can have different value and purpose. Some data is most valuable at the time it is collected. After some time, their value decreases rapidly.

Other data is designed to accumulate a certain amount of data in order to make analytics based on it relevant.

Edge Computing and Fog systems allow data to be analysed before it is sent to the central Cloud, at a time when its value is maximised. For example, a hacker attack or system intrusion can be prevented more effectively when the analysis happens right at the point of attack or intrusion. Waiting for the data to be sent to the central data centre takes precious time.

Therefore, extracting the part of the total, large amount of data that should be transferred to the Cloud (Data thinning) and cutting off unnecessary data is a very important process that separates valuable data from low-value data. For example, an unmanned car generates a lot of intermediate data that does not need to be stored in a data centre for a long time.

Fog computing also helps to solve the data problems of industrial robots. The vast majority of this data is needed only at the place where the robot is working, so it is more efficient and expedient to process it there. Drones that explore the earth's landscape for various purposes (security, agriculture, monitoring pipelines and power lines, etc.) also generate a huge amount of data that is needed in a very short time. Transferring this data to a central cloud is very costly and often technically impossible, and waiting for commands from the centre is wasted time. All that is required of such devices is to recognise the images perceived by machine vision, collect meaningful data and send that data to the people who need that data at that moment in time. For example, drones could be used in agriculture to assess the need to irrigate fields and, if such a need is detected, notify the farmer by sending him an image of a field with areas that need to be irrigated urgently, areas that can be irrigated after a while, and areas that do not need to be irrigated soon.

Table 2.1 shows the main differences in requirements between Cloud and Fog Computing systems.

Table 2.1. Differences in requirements for Cloud and Fog systems (source: Cisco).

Requirements	Cloud Computing	Fog Computing
Data delay	High	Low
Delay jitter	High	Very low
Location of the service software	On the Internet	At the edge of the network
Distance between client and server	Lots of transitions	One hop
Safety	It's hard to ask	You can set
Data interception during transmission	High probability	Very low probability
Geographical distribution	Centralised	Local
Number of server nodes	A few	Very much so.
Mobility support	Restricted	Supported by
Support for real-time interaction	Supported by	Supported by
Last Mile Connectivity Type	Dedicated line	Wireless network

Table 2.2 shows the main problems of Cloud and how they are solved in Fog.

Table 2.2. Key Cloud issues and Fog solutions (source: Cisco).

Cloud	Fog
Data and applications are processed in a centralised Cloud, which takes a lot of time if the data volume is large.	Instead of sending data to the centre, it is processed at the edge of the network, so processing time is significantly reduced.
The problem of lack of bandwidth as a result of sending the full amount of data to be processed to a centralised Cloud Cloud Cloud	Less network bandwidth requirement of aggregation and core layers, due to the fact that data bits are aggregated at Fog nodes and partially processed there, with redundant data removed.
Slow response and scaling issues as a result of remotely located servers.	Placing small servers, called edge servers, close to users in the Fog network avoids the response latency problem and solves the scaling problem.

Four main reasons for the need for Fog computing can be formulated:

1. Fog provides real-time processing and control of CPS (cyber-physical system) cyber-physical systems;

2. Fog helps applications can meet the requirements of users;

3. Fog provides an environment for pooling local resources (i.e., flexibly reassigning and reusing them in local systems);

4. Fog enables rapid innovation and scaling at an affordable cost.

It can be concluded that Fog has advantages over Cloud, however, it cannot completely replace centralised Cloud. Cloud centralised cloud will be preferred in case of massive and multi-threaded computing, the need for which remains high.

Fog and Cloud will complement each other and at the same time each of these paradigms will have its own advantages and disadvantages. Fog and the closely related concept of Edge computing will play a critical role in the development of the Internet of Things (IoT).

Fog computing will grow due to the emergence of new networking paradigms with requirements for fast processing with lower latency and jitter. Cloud computing will serve the purposes of high performance computing, processing large amounts of heterogeneous data at the core of artificial intelligence, long-term storage of data whose value either does not diminish or falls relatively slowly over time.

Cloud technologies in education

The "Strategy for the Development of Information Society for 2017-2030" defines the concept of "cloud computing" as follows: "a model of information technology that provides ubiquitous and convenient access via the Internet to a common set of customisable computing resources ("cloud")". Thus, the virtual cloud is a provider of remote computing resources and services at the request of the consumer. Despite the relative novelty of cloud computing, there is already experience of its use in the educational process. For example, some foreign and domestic educational institutions use cloud services provided by Microsoft Live @ edu, Google Apps, etc. Another cloud service that is beginning to spread in the field of education is moving Learning Management Systems (LMS) to the cloud.

At present, the cloud service Office 365 of Microsoft Corporation, which includes a cloud version of Microsoft Office (Outlook, Word, Excel, Power Point, OneNote Web Apps), as well as collaboration tools (Lync Online, SharePoint Online and Exchange Online), is being widely implemented in educational institutions of our country. The introduction of this cloud-based service into the educational process has enhanced the possibilities of mobile work and increased the efficiency, reliability and security of the system.

Cloud technologies involve running applications or storing data on servers located in distributed data centres (DCs) accessible via the Internet. The development and implementation of such applications requires a dedicated cloud platform. Such a platform is Windows Azure, the cloud analogue of the Windows Server operating system. Unlike Windows Server, the Windows Azure platform is hosted in Microsoft data centres and is available to you remotely as an environment for developing and running applications. At the same time, there is no need to buy and install the corresponding software, but simply pay for the lease of computing resources and capacity of the Microsoft data centre platform.

Windows Azure application in education provides teachers with an opportunity to incorporate one of the most innovative and rapidly developing technologies - cloud computing - into the educational process, both in theoretical and practical terms, to create virtual computer labs. The use of these technologies allows students and teachers to get remote access to the resources and services of the educational institution using various means of communication (computers, tablets, smartphones). Having analysed the experience of using cloud computing, we can conclude that most educational institutions use the cloud model as software. The use of this model does not require an educational institution to create its own server and its maintenance, it avoids economic and organisational costs and allows installing its own applications on the platform provided by the cloud service provider.

Widely used educational cloud PaaS service

(Platform as a Service) is the Education Cloud portal (http://ooblako.ru/). The concept of the Education Cloud provides for the creation of a digital educational environment that aims to improve communication and co-operation between the parties of education.

Cloud Education provides learners and educators with access to educational databases and information systems that support teaching and administrative activities in educational institutions. Through Cloud Education, you can easily access digital educational materials and services based on modern IT technologies.

Educational Cloud is a tool for creating electronic learning resources (ESM) for the organisation of online and distance learning, especially relevant at the moment due to the spread of coronavirus infection. The following advantages of using the Education Cloud can be emphasised:

1) creation of electronic learning resources (e-Learning resources);

2) creation of training courses based on electronic learning modules (ELMs);

3) implementation of educational activities with the use of eLMs and e-Learning resources;

4) training using the developed elements;

5) exchange of experience between teachers.

As an example of the use of cloud technologies in education, we can name e-journals, e-classrooms, thematic forums (where information can be exchanged).

Using Cloud Education allows certain learning tasks to be carried out even in the absence of a teacher or under the supervision of a teacher. You can use it for this purpose:
1) computer programmes;
2) e-textbooks;
3) simulators;
4) diagnostic, testing and training systems;
5) software applications and tools;
6) virtual laboratory complexes;
7) systems based on multimedia technology;
8) telecommunication systems (e.g. e-mail, teleconferencing);
9) digital libraries, etc.

Cloud technologies offer an alternative to traditional forms of organising the learning process, creating opportunities for personal learning, interactive classes, team teaching, distance learning, creating web-oriented laboratories in specific subject areas. Implementation of joint projects in groups: preparation of text files and presentations, organisation of discussion of changes in documents in real time with other co-authors, publication of the results of work on the Internet in the form of publicly accessible web pages, performance of practical tasks on processing of information objects of various kinds: formatting and editing of text, creation of tables and diagrams in a text editor. Such opportunities are provided through the use of free Google Docs (Documents and Presentations) services. The use of these services will allow educational institutions to create a unified information infrastructure. Google Docs (Tables) service allows you to create summary tables and diagrams to analyse statistical data. It is possible to carry out both individual and joint practical work on modelling.

Cloud technologies in medicine

Cloud technologies are becoming more and more firmly embedded in various spheres of life. In recent years, the cloud medical information system has experienced a real "boom" - experts estimate that this industry could grow by more than $25 billion in the coming year.

Healthcare has always had to work with large data sets, and until recently they were stored in paper archives. This approach caused a lot of inconvenience for both doctors and patients. Searching for necessary documents often took a lot of time, and their storage required additional space. In addition, there was no information link between different medical institutions, which did not allow data to be transferred directly.

All this has led to the need to introduce new technologies into the medical industry. However, with the beginning of digitisation of all data, new difficulties arose. It turned out that data in this form also required a large amount of resources for storage. Using in-house server equipment proved to be too costly and as inconvenient as possible. In addition, the problem of digital communication between the various clinics and hospitals arose again.

But with the development of cloud technologies it was possible to solve a number of problems and create an effective and convenient information system for managing the medical sphere. Let us tell you about the main features of using cloud-technologies in healthcare.

Creating a single profile for each patient

One of the biggest trends in the development of medical cloud systems has been the creation of a single digital profile for each patient. The cloud has made it possible to set up regular data exchange between different medical institutions, regulators and even patients. Almost all countries have already launched their own projects to form a single space for data exchange between private and public clinics.

In Russia, this area is dealt with by the Ministry of Health. As part of the work on the project, the EGISZ system was created. It includes 13 subsystems and registers, which are integrated into a single network. All the system data is placed in the cloud, which helps to solve the issue of database storage, as well as to speed up the creation of machine learning models.

It is worth noting that cloud technologies are fully compliant with federal laws on the processing of personal data. This is a mandatory requirement for hospitals, laboratories and medical centres - organisations work with sensitive data (e.g. patient contact information, medical records, etc.), so they must comply with legal regulations. The medical industry uses cloud-based platforms that comply with FSTEC UZ-1 requirements to store databases.

Automatic scaling

The use of cloud-based solutions has allowed clinics and laboratories to adapt their own infrastructure to current workloads.

In recent years, the pandemic has resulted in increased laboratory workloads for many health care facilities. The number of coronavirus tests in some clinics has been as high as 10,000 per day, and there has been an increased need for lung CT scans and various tests to determine complications of COVID-19. All this could not but affect the IT infrastructure of the clinics.

And, as practice has shown, the institutions that have already used cloud technologies have coped with the new needs much better. The fact is that the cloud allows for almost instant scaling of the system, and in some cases - to make this process automatic. In the face of unpredictable workloads, the cloud has made it possible to avoid disruptions and keep tasks running smoothly.

Improving the quality of surveys

If we talk about the cloud for medicine, it is impossible not to mention the benefits for diagnosing various diseases. The introduction of new technologies has made it possible to create new approaches in the field of examinations.

For example, the Medical Decision Support System has become a standard in healthcare. Thanks to artificial intelligence, a doctor can use a greater number of hypotheses. AI is able to diagnose diseases by collecting, analysing and systematising patient data and correlating anamnesis with examination results.

The positive impact of AI and cloud technology has been noted in the field of radiology. New technologies help doctors to read radiological images correctly and quickly and to virtualise them. Many medical software companies are already moving to the cloud to speed up the process of integrating systems in clinics. As a result, even medical centres in remote areas have been able to access databases and join a common standard for diagnosing diseases.

Effective communication with patients

Many patients today are actively using new technologies, including various mobile tools, apps and programmes. Therefore, medical centres and hospitals are increasingly looking for new communication channels.

One of the results of the development of cloud-based medical infrastructure has been the introduction of chatbots and the use of automated call centres.

Today's patients are actively using mobile tools. This allows medical centres, hospitals and other organisations to seek new communication channels. Increasingly, the healthcare industry has started to use tools to automate call centres and introduce chatbots.

And in 2020, during the spring self-isolation, the Ministry of Health of the Moscow region launched an informer robot that monitored citizens in quarantine. Such a robot was able to clarify the well-being of patients and, if necessary, transfer the call to a doctor or ambulance. The informant also gave practical advice on signing up at the MFC, getting an electronic sick leave or applying for financial support.

Cloud technology in a pandemic

If we talk about the speed of cloud medicine development, it increased with the onset of the coronavirus pandemic. Of course, it's too early to talk about the "results" of the epidemic, but it appears that the healthcare industry has become one of the few to survive the growth.

In a period of mandatory social distancing and the imposition of a number of restrictions, healthcare providers have had to rethink the interaction between doctors and patients. This led to the rapid development of such a field as telehealth. According to the most conservative estimates of experts, technology adoption has accelerated almost twofold.

The full development of telemedicine requires a well-functioning IT infrastructure that allows quick access to any patient information. For this purpose, IaaS-platforms - an effective cloud computing model that allows access to the required capacities in the cloud - have been used. Such a solution allows an unlimited number of users from any region to work simultaneously in the service.

Benefits of using cloud computing

The use of cloud-technologies in healthcare has solved many problems and difficulties. For example, new solutions have improved the quality of patient care and the efficiency of doctors' work in a rather tight schedule. Treatment has become more competent and diagnoses, thanks to AI, more accurate.

When it comes to the benefits of cloud computing, it's worth noting:

• **Data storage**. The cloud has made it possible to solve the problems of storing electronic medical records of patients, test results and other information. Such information requires special processing and storage, and not all equipment is suitable for this. Cloud resources allow medical centres to store all records, avoiding the cost of physical servers.

• **Scalability**. Unlike traditional medical database hosting models, cloud computing offers the ability to reduce or increase storage capacity. This may be necessary during peak times (e.g. during the autumn cold and flu season).

• **Security**. Years of experience with cloud-based systems have shown that they are as reliable and secure as traditional models. What's more, the use of cloud technology can improve data security and backup.

• **Cost optimisation**. Medical organisations can save money on the purchase of expensive equipment and systems. In addition, clinics can further reduce costs by utilising the resources of a cloud service provider.

Conclusions

Cloud technology in medicine still has a long way to go. It is necessary to combine such computing with artificial intelligence and other emerging technologies. There is also a need for further development in the area of data analytics.

However, it can already be said that the use of cloud-based solutions can increase the efficiency of medical services and open up new opportunities for their optimisation and development. New technologies increase the accessibility of services for patients and at the same time reduce the costs of medical institutions.

Cloud technologies in business

The penetration of cloud technologies could not fail to affect business: according to MegaFon's report, 66% of companies have already transferred IT tasks to the cloud by at least half. The majority of companies made the digital transition in the last 2.5 years, and 53% implemented cloud solutions less than two years ago, and their number is growing every day.

In response to this growing demand, a range of services and turnkey solutions have emerged to ease the transition to the cloud for businesses of all sizes. This has also made cloud technology for business even more popular and affordable, shattering the myth that it is expensive for businesses and only suitable for large corporations.

Mid-sized and small businesses need cloud technology more than ever, but unlike large companies, they are focusing on the cost of cloud solutions and only then on performance and functionality. Right now, the cloud is becoming a key tool in the fight for survival in a competitive market - that's why it's so important to consider adopting it today.

Why small and medium-sized businesses need it

The unfavourable epidemiological situation has forced even the most conservative companies to reorganise. This has led to a significant increase in requests for organising remote workplaces and building cloud platforms that are ready to scale and expand.

Two years ago, MegaFon launched its own multifunctional cloud platform, MegaFon Cloud, and the sale of solutions for organising remote workplaces. Using the cloud, customers automatically receive all the advantages of cloud solutions: fault tolerance, availability, and support. The advantages of MegaFon's solutions are the speed of deployment of remote workplaces. For example, it takes only one day to prepare the cloud infrastructure and only a few minutes to create secure access to workplaces.

More and more employees are being forced to work remotely, which means different companies are faced with the same challenges every day of keeping important departments running smoothly and providing employees with convenient tools. Even if an office consists of ten working computers, as a company grows and evolves, it will need more capacity, additional software and specialists to maintain and support the system.

To keep all the systems that power your business running properly, it's important to be able to calculate how much hardware you need and predict how much you'll need as your needs grow. Cloud technology provides exactly the amount of resources you need today or right now, allowing you to focus on your business-critical tasks. The most important advantage is that you can pay only for the services you use and only for the capacity you use, not for everything at once.

What services are available to small and medium-sized businesses

Versatility, flexibility and speed of implementation are the main advantages of cloud technologies. Off-the-shelf solutions allow you to move your current tasks to the cloud in the easiest, most efficient and painless way for your business. You can start small: gradually moving one or two departments, setting up access to cloud storage, and deploying corporate email and messengers.

MegaFon's Platform for Business solution includes the most popular SaaS services required by small and medium-sized companies: corporate mail and corporate messenger, cloud storage of files and documents. Through a single interface, the platform provides access to a set of services for corporate communications, cloud storage and company marketing. Additional services can be purchased as needed, and you only pay for what you really need.

As your needs grow, it is possible to increase speed, power, performance or other required features. Powerful servers provide uninterrupted operation for all connected devices. Medium and small business owners often spend money on server room equipment that requires component upgrades every few years. With cloud solutions, this is no longer necessary. Information is stored on a cloud server, so your business is not at risk.

"MegaFon Cloud" also offers advanced data protection against data theft and DDo S attacks to ensure uninterrupted operation. The platform meets the information security requirements for personal data information systems of the first level of security in accordance with Federal Law No. 152 "On Personal Data", which is confirmed by the relevant certificate. The data is located in a protected circuit, which ensures fulfilment of all legal requirements for processing and protection of personal data.

How it is good for business and what benefits it brings

According to Accenture, the majority of surveyed companies see an increase in financial performance when switching to the cloud model. This is confirmed by a recent study by MegaFon: revenue increase by 53%, cost reduction by 64%, and competitiveness growth by 69%.

The use of IaaS and SaaS services, the predominant consumers of which are small and medium-sized businesses, leads to cost reduction. According to MegaFon's data, more than 20 per cent of companies reported a reduction in

IT services, personnel and energy costs after implementing cloud technologies.

Optimisation of hardware and software costs, convenient access to large capacities and no need to search for specialists when buying off-the-shelf solutions allow small and medium-sized businesses to keep up with the times.

According to a survey of more than 100 companies, half of which are small businesses, 29% of respondents believe that clouds are cheaper than building and maintaining their own infrastructure. Among the advantages, 43% of specialists identified virtually unlimited resources and ready-made infrastructure, 30% - the ability to quickly scale computing resources, and 23% of respondents are attracted by the model of payment only for consumed capacity.

According to MegaFon's report, 90% of companies are already satisfied with the effect of using cloud technologies. IT productivity growth and the speed of launching new products and services on the market increases by 30% after switching to the cloud.

An undeniable advantage of cloud solutions is the ability to create cloud access terminals using existing computers, without the cost of retrofitting. Maintaining server rooms, constantly maintaining and upgrading equipment becomes impractical, as well as paying for space and additional electricity. You can expand and strengthen your business without physically expanding, overpaying for rent or buying new equipment. All the potential of employees can be directed to solving business tasks and developing the company, while the employees themselves can be located anywhere.

Properly assembled architecture at the level of computing platform infrastructure, competently selected information security components, regulated access, prepared performance level - all this together makes clouds the most optimal choice in terms of price/performance ratio.

qualities. The cloud can be both expensive and cheap, but the right answer is that the cloud costs exactly what your business needs.

The evolution of the cloud

The cloud has also prompted a number of other service providers to modify their products and expand their business strategies to accommodate changing buyer behaviour in IT for business.

For example, HPE, Dell and VMware were initially going to go head-to-head with Amazon, Google and Microsoft before discontinuing their public cloud service initiatives, citing competitive pressures.

While some have dropped out of the game altogether, VMware and

Rackspace have taken a slightly different route, with both positioning themselves as organisations that can help enterprises manage applications and workloads in their competitors' public clouds.

In Rackspace's case, this has led to the fact that, having started with early market leadership in the IaaS to AWS market, since 2015 (or so) the company's focus has shifted to helping enterprises manage their cloud deployments on Amazon, Microsoft, Google and others.

This refocus has paid off for the firm, and AWS service desk is regularly cited by the company as one of the fastest growing parts of the business.

At the same time, VMware, while remaining one of the market leaders in virtualisation software, sold its public cloud business to French IaaS competitor, OVH, in April 2017. VMware is now positioning itself as a hybrid cloud provider.

What's next for the cloud?

In light of all this, it's fair to say that the next 10 years are likely to be just as busy for cloud technology as corporate appetites for the technology (and their expectations of how it benefits their organisations) continue to grow.

The major barriers to cloud adoption are now almost a thing of the past, as previously perceived weaknesses such as security are now often seen as strengths.

Cloud technologies are now generating huge revenues for cloud service providers and technology vendors. Researchers predict that the current market growth rate will decline quite slowly over the next five years.

Russian corporate cloud provider Cloud4Y was founded in 2009 - we were one of the first to pioneer cloud services among Russian providers who are familiar with the specifics and meet the needs of Russian business. Today the company is among the top 8 largest IaaS providers in Russia 2017 and the top 11 leaders of the rating of SaaS providers in Russia according to Cnews Analytics.

Network models of cloud computing
Hosting cloud applications

When discussing cloud computing, one should pay attention to where applications are located. There are currently three main models of application location:
- in the customer's infrastructure;
- from the host company;
- in the cloud.

Deployment at the customer's infrastructure (*on premises*). This is the most traditional model of application deployment and has been around for decades. On-premises deployment involves a significant upfront investment in hardware, software, network infrastructure, and personnel.

This model - pay, acquire, own - is directly related to high capital costs, but it also provides full control over infrastructure, hardware and software.

Hosted by a host company (*hosting*). This model of application deployment, formerly called *Application Services Prodiver* (*ASP*) and then *SaaS* or simply "hosting", was developed a few years ago and is one of the most popular ways to reduce IT costs. It is based on renting a hardware platform, software, the associated infrastructure and the staff to maintain it. This model is characterised by less control over infrastructure, hardware and software and is based on payment for a fixed number of resources, which usually implies payment even when the leased resources are not used.

Location in the *cloud*. This model has emerged quite recently. It involves payment on the basis of the actual use of leased hardware and software resources, which leads to a significant reduction in upfront costs and a transition from capital investment to operating expenses. This model is characterised by virtually no control over the infrastructure and hardware, and in the case of software leasing - even no control over it.

Each approach has its advantages and disadvantages, but, from an economic perspective, the most important characteristic is the pay-as-you-go nature of cloud computing.

Cloud computing is an approach to the hosting, provisioning and consumption of applications and computing resources in which applications and resources are made available over the Internet as services consumed across multiple platforms and devices. Payment for such services is based on their actual use.

Network models of cloud computing

There are four different cloud models that can be subscribed to according to business needs (Figure 4.1).

A private cloud is an enterprise's internal cloud infrastructure and services. These clouds are located within the corporate network. An organisation can manage the private cloud itself or outsource this task. The infrastructure can be hosted either on the customer's premises or by an external operator, or partly by the customer and partly by the operator.

	Private Cloud
	Community Cloud
	Public Cloud
	Hybrid Cloud

Figure 4.1. Four cloud computing models

The ideal private cloud is a cloud deployed on premises, maintained and monitored by the organisation's employees.

Private clouds offer the same advantages as public clouds, but with one important feature: the enterprise is responsible for installing and maintaining the cloud itself. The complexity and cost of setting up an internal cloud can be very high, and the cost of running it can exceed the cost of using public clouds.

It should be noted that private clouds have advantages over public clouds: more granular control over the various cloud resources provides the company with any available configuration options. In addition, private clouds are ideal when you need to perform work that cannot be entrusted to a public cloud for security reasons.

A community cloud is a type of infrastructure designed for use by a specific community of consumers from organisations that share a common mission. A community cloud may be cooperatively owned, managed and operated by one or more of the community organisations or a third party (or some combination thereof), and it may exist physically inside or outside the owner's jurisdiction. This type of infrastructure is mainly used for security reasons.

Public clouds are infrastructure designed for free use by the general public. They are located outside the corporate network. Users of these clouds do not have the ability to manage or maintain the cloud, all responsibility rests with the owner of the cloud. **The cloud provider assumes the responsibility of installing, managing, provisioning and maintaining the software,**

application infrastructure or physical infrastructure. Customers pay only for the resources they use.

The services offered can be subscribed to by any company or individual user. They offer an easy and affordable way to deploy websites or business systems with great scalability that would not be available in other solutions. **Examples: Amazon EC2 and Amazon Simple Storage Service (S3) online services, Google Apps/Docs, Salesforce.com, Microsoft Office Web.** However, public cloud services are mostly provided in the form of standardised configurations, i.e. based on the conditions of the most common use cases. This means that the user has fewer configuration choices compared to systems where resources are managed by the consumer. It should also be borne in mind that because consumers have little control over the infrastructure, processes that require stringent security and compliance measures are not always suitable for implementation in the public cloud.

A hybrid cloud is a combination of two or more different cloud infrastructures (private, public or community). They are typically built by the enterprise and management responsibilities are shared between the enterprise and the public cloud provider. Hybrid cloud provides services, some of which are public and some of which are private. Typically, this type of cloud is used when an organisation has seasonal periods of activity. In other words, as soon as the internal IT infrastructure cannot cope with the current tasks, part of the capacity is moved to the public cloud (e.g., large amounts of statistical information that in its raw form is of no value to the enterprise), and to provide users with access to enterprise resources (to the private cloud) via the public cloud. A well-designed hybrid cloud can serve both security-critical processes, such as receiving payments from customers, as well as more non-essential processes.

The main disadvantage of this type of cloud is the difficulty of effectively creating and managing such solutions. You need to obtain services from different sources and organise them as if they were a single source. The interaction between the private and public components can further complicate the solution. As this is a relatively new architectural concept in cloud computing, more and more practical guidelines and tools are emerging for this model, and its widespread adoption may be delayed until it is better understood.

According to Tom Bittman, vice president and lead analyst at Gartner, a U.S. research and consulting firm, among the three cloud deployment models listed above, private clouds are the most relevant to businesses right now. **Bittman highlighted five key points that help to get a more accurate**

picture of the private cloud.

Cloud is not just about virtualisation. While server and infrastructure virtualisation form an important foundation of private cloud computing, virtualisation and the management of a virtualised environment are not yet private clouds in themselves.

Virtualisation allows for better structuring, pooling and dynamic provisioning of infrastructure resources: servers, desktops, storage capacity, networking equipment, connectivity software, etc. But in order for an environment to be technically considered a cloud environment, you need other components such as virtual machines, operating systems or containers of middleware, highly resilient operating systems, grid computing software, storage abstraction software, scaling and clustering tools.

The term private cloud, as opposed to public or hybrid cloud, refers to resources used by a single organisation, or means that an organisation's cloud resources are completely isolated in the cloud from the rest of the organisation.

The cloud is not necessarily a source of savings. One of the major misconceptions is that the cloud will save money. Savings are possible, but not a necessary attribute.

Private cloud allows for more efficient reallocation of resources to meet corporate requirements and can reduce capital expenditure on hardware. But private cloud requires investment in automation, and the savings alone may not pay for the entire cost. So, cost reduction is not the main benefit of this model. From this point of view, the main incentive for adopting the cloud model should not be savings, but speed to market, the ability to quickly adapt and dynamically scale according to demand, which can increase the speed of new service deployment.

Private cloud is not always implemented at the customer's premises. Private cloud means privacy, not specific location, resource ownership or self-management. Many vendors offer non-local private clouds, meaning they allocate resources to a single customer, precluding multiple customers from sharing a single pool. "A cloud is called private by its privacy, not by where it's deployed, who owns it, or who is responsible for managing it," Bittman emphasises. Some, for example, may host their data centres with hosting providers or pool resources from different customers **but isolate them from each other using Virtual Private Network (VPN) and other similar technologies.**

Private cloud (like public cloud) is not just about infrastructure services.

Server virtualisation is a major trend and therefore a powerful driver of private cloud computing. But private cloud is not just about **infrastructure-as-a-service (IaaS).** For example, for developing and testing new software, a high-level Platform as a **Service (PaaS)** makes more sense than just providing virtual machines.

Today, the fastest growing segment of cloud computing is IaaS. It provides the lowest-level data centre resources in an easy-to-use form, but does not fundamentally change the way things work. To create new applications that are originally designed for the cloud and provide completely new services that may be very different from what previous applications provided, developers are more comfortable using PaaS.

The private cloud may no longer be private. On the one hand, the private cloud offers the advantages of the cloud: speed of rebuilding, scalability and efficiency, and avoids some of the security threats, potential and real, that are inherent in public clouds. On the other hand, service levels, security and compliance controls in public cloud services will certainly increase over time. Therefore, some private clouds will probably migrate to the public cloud category entirely. Most private cloud services, however, are likely to evolve into hybrid cloud services, expanding the available capabilities by leveraging public cloud services and other third-party resources.

Key characteristics of cloud technologies

NIST (National Institute of Standards and Technology, USA) in its document "The NIST Definition of Cloud Computing" defines the following characteristics of clouds: scalability, elasticity, multitenancy, pay-per-use and self-service.

Scalability. The introduction of new products and services, expansion of the sales channel and the number of customers require an organisation's information systems to withstand growing loads and process large volumes of data. Fast and reliable performance that eliminates denials of service, delays in system responses, and failures can increase customer loyalty and satisfaction. A scalable application can handle more load by increasing the number of instances running simultaneously. Typical hardware is used to run multiple instances simultaneously, reducing total cost of ownership and simplifying infrastructure maintenance.

Elasticity. Flexible response to changing business conditions is one of the characteristics of a successful business. For example, prevailing market conditions and competitors' actions may require the rapid introduction of a new product or service, while carrying out a full cycle of planning, design and development of IS. Elasticity allows the capacity of the infrastructure to ramp up quickly, without the need to make initial investments in hardware and software. Elasticity is related to application scalability, as it solves the problem of instantaneous changes in the amount of computing resources allocated for IS operation.

Multitenancy is one of the ways to reduce costs by maximising the use of shared resources to serve different groups of users, different organisations, different categories of consumers, and others. Multitenancy can be particularly attractive for application development companies, as it allows them to reduce their own costs of paying for cloud platform resources and maximise the use of available computing resources.

Pay-per-use. Pay-per-use is another attribute of cloud computing that allows you to shift some of your capital costs to operational costs. By purchasing only the amount of resources required, the costs associated with running an organisation's IP can be optimised. And when combined with multitenancy, by sharing resources between different consumers, it is possible to reduce costs even further. Elasticity will allow you to quickly change the amount of resources up or down, thereby bringing IT costs in line with the actual needs of the organisation.

Self-service. Rapid market launch of a new product or service in modern conditions is accompanied by deployment or modification of IS. Traditionally, IP deployment is preceded by hardware specification, procurement and configuration. Depending on who performs the application development process (contractor or in-house), it may require the allocation of hardware resources and software installation. All of this can take a long time: months or even years. Self-service allows consumers to request and receive the required resources in minutes.

As can be seen, only the combination of several attributes of cloud computing leads to the achievement of the objective of increasing revenues and reducing costs. Thus, paying only for the resources used is maximised when combined with the elasticity of the infrastructure.

Elasticity, in turn, assumes that applications are scalable, otherwise rapid resource allocation will not lead to improved performance.

We have seen above how the key attributes of cloud computing can have an impact on an organisation's ability to increase revenue and reduce costs. It should also be understood that moving to the cloud is not a trivial task and often requires reviewing and changing the architecture of existing solutions, and sometimes completely abandoning them in favour of creating new ones that are tailored to the capabilities provided by cloud platforms. Depending on the architecture of existing applications and the technologies on which they are implemented, their migration to a cloud platform may result in a number of benefits, or it may lead to additional challenges, such as interoperability or limitations of implementing a server platform at the cloud level. As one step in adapting cloud computing, we can consider moving to a service-oriented architecture.

Examples of cloud platforms

When discussing the different types of cloud services - software, platform and infrastructure-as-a-service - attention should be paid to the so-called manageability boundaries - i.e., what can be managed when moving to a cloud platform compared to traditional models of deployment in-house.

For obvious reasons, infrastructure-as-a-service provides great opportunities to customise individual components, whereas platform-as-a-service and software-as-a-service practically minimise these opportunities.

When you deploy your own infrastructure, you need to manage all its components - from network resources to running applications. Whereas with the *IaaS* model, you can control components such as code execution environment, security and integration, databases, and others. When moving to a *PaaS* model, all the components of the platform are provided as services with limited ability to manage them. This is done to provide customers with an optimally configured platform that does not require additional customisation.

Existing cloud platforms

There are many cloud computing platforms on the market today. There are both proprietary (commercial) and open (free) platforms. Based on open platforms, such as *OpenStack, Cloud Foundry*, many companies create their own infrastructures and offer tools for their management, in particular, provide complexes for turning existing resources into clouds.

In order to choose the most suitable platform and provider, you need to clearly articulate your cloud requirements and trial and error testing of all possible platforms.

Some of the most active and serious players in the cloud computing market are the following platforms and companies:

Amazon Web Services.

Amazon is the pioneer of the cloud platform market, and today it is the undisputed market leader. The peculiarity of *AWS* is that it is an infrastructure service (*IaaS*), which provides maximum freedom to developers in the choice of platform and development environment. *AWS is* suitable for hosting corporate applications and content, as well as for building *SaaS* services.

- ▶ provides IaaS, PaaS services;
- ▶ Elastic Compute Cloud (EC2) scalable servers for computing;
- ▶ Elastic MapReduce (EMR) analytics;
- ▶ Simple Storage Service (S3) webservice based data storage;
- ▶ DynamoDB, SimpleDB databases.

Google App Engine + Google Apps:

The *Google App Engine* platform has a humane attitude towards startups - it provides limited free resources (disc space and traffic), which are very useful for *SaaS* start-ups. *GAE* supports only two programming languages so far - *Python* and *Java. GAE is* mainly focused on creating *SaaS* services for small businesses. In addition to the infrastructure platform, *Google* provides a set of *APIs* for integrating the service with popular *Google Apps* applications and the *Google Apps Marketplace* to bring your service to the market.

- ▶ Provides PaaS services;
- ▶ automatic scaling depending on the number of requests;
- ▶ Java (+ others using JVM, e.g. Scala), Python, Go and PHP are supported;
- ▶ limited list of APIs: BigTable database, HTTP requests, image processing

Microsoft Azure:

It is an ideal cloud platform for Microsoft-centric developers and companies. However, *Windows Azure* also supports *PHP*, *MySQL*, *Ruby on Rails*, *Python, Java, Eclipse* and *Zend.* The main advantage of *Azure* over *Amazon Web Services* and *Rackspace Cloud* is its high level of automation. In addition, this platform allows easy integration of hosted applications with the local IT infrastructure of the company using *SOAP, REST* and *XML* standards.

- ▶ provides PaaS and IaaS services;
- ▶ managing virtual machines running Windows Server and Linux;
- ▶ SQL Azure database (cloud version of MS SQL Server);
- ▶ web applications based on ASP.NET, PHP, Node.js, Python;
- ▶ analytics using available SDKs, particularly Hadoop and machine learning.

This platform will be discussed in more detail in the next section.

Force.com.

Salesforce's platform, *Force. com* - claims to be a monopolist in the market of enterprise *SaaS* applications. The platform is built around the most successful enterprise SaaS16 system - *Salesforce* and allows you to create add-ons to this system or independent applications. *Force.com* provides a wide range of development tools (*Apex, Flash, Java*), interface builder, ready-made modules (authentication, social tools, business processes, analytics) and application supermarket with a huge user base.

VMWare vCloud

VMWare vCloud is not a self-sufficient cloud platform.

This is an intermediate layer that several *VMWare* partners provide on top of their server infrastructure (*Salesforce is the* latest to join the list of partners). *VMWare is* the global market leader in virtualisation systems, so the main advantage of this platform is support for virtual application images. In particular, it allows to quickly and easily migrate local business applications to the cloud platform without the problems associated with the migration of the associated IT infrastructure.

IBM Cloud

IBM Cloud is mainly focused on large companies and resource-intensive processes: software development and testing, storage and analytical processing of huge data sets. Obviously, after the recent acquisition of the *OmniConnect* service, another function of this cloud will be the integration of disparate cloud systems and platforms.

Heroku:

▶ Provides PaaS services;

▶ web and command line interface for most operations, support for quickly adding modules (Heroku Elements);

▶ support for Ruby, Java, JavaScript / Node.js, Scala, Clojure, Python, PHP;

▶ PostgreSQL (relational), MongoDB, Redis (non-relational) databases.

Thus, there are enough platforms on the market for there to be a choice.

Data storage services

There are quite a lot of cloud storages, and they all provide different features. They are: paid and free, designed for large amounts of information and small amounts, support for different operating systems, etc. The only thing they are similar in is the way they process information. Some of the most popular cloud storages are:

Dropbox is a cloud storage service that allows users to store their data on servers in the cloud and share it with others on the internet. Its operation is based on data synchronisation. The Dropbox app can be downloaded and installed on a PC, Mac, Linux or mobile device. One of the main advantages of Dropbox is that it is easy and intuitive to use - you just need to upload files to a Dropbox folder, publish it, or synchronise it with the right device. The service keeps a history of uploads, so that after deleting files from the server it is possible to restore the data. The history of files changes is also kept, which is available for the period of the last 30 days.

Google Drive is a free cloud storage service that allows users to store their data on servers in the cloud and share it with other users on the Internet. Google Drive is characterised by a concise interface and offers to install convenient software clients for smartphones and tablets based on the Android operating system, PCs and laptops running Windows or MacOS, iPhone and iPad mobile devices. In the future, the storage is expected to be more tightly integrated with Chrome OS and support for Linux. Each Google Drive user gets up to 15 GB of free space for all Google services (including Gmail and Photos). At the same time, he can decide how much space to allocate for mail and how much space to leave for important files. You can work with files in Google Drive right in your browser. Google Drive can be turned into a separate folder in the documents of your smartphone, tablet or PC, and its contents will be synchronised automatically. Once activated, it replaces Google Docs. In the new service you can store not only documents, but also photos, music, videos and many other files - a total of 30 types. But in general, everything is very convenient and familiar to users of Google services.

Google Docs is a free online office that includes a word processor, a spreadsheet processor, a presentation creation service, and a cloud-based online file storage service with file sharing features. It allows you to create and edit standard documents, spreadsheets and presentations, and supports collaboration features.

Mega (MEGA Encrypted Global Access) is an ambitious newcomer, a cloud file sharing service by Kim Dotcom, founder of the legendary Megaupload. Mega is undoubtedly one of the most profitable cloud services in terms of disc space and its cost, besides, an important difference between Mega and other similar services is privacy, as Mega is positioned as a service that protects the user's personal data. However, there are still some shortcomings, in particular, Mega still loses to other flagships of cloud data storage in synchronisation with different devices.

Yandex.Disk is a free cloud service from Yandex that allows users to store their data on servers in the cloud and transfer it to other users on the Internet. The work is based on synchronising data between different devices. Yandex.Disk can act as a cloud service, integrating into the Microsoft Office 2013 office suite, and recently it has become possible to automatically upload photos and video files from digital cameras and external storage media.

Облако@Маil.ru is a product of a Russian company. A new and very promising cloud data storage service from Mail.Ru Group, allowing users to store their data in the cloud and synchronise data on different devices, as well as share it with other users. Облако@таП.ш provides a large amount of disc space for free. Users can immediately get 25GB of cloud storage for free. This product is subject to the Mail.ru rule for mailboxes. If you do not use it for three months, the account is cancelled along with all the contents. The service application is available not only through the web-interface, but also for personal computers and laptops with Windows, Linux and Mac. There are mobile applications for iOS, Android and Windows Phone. A feature that has been available in mobile apps from the very beginning is autoloading photos from your phone. When enabled, all photos taken with your device are instantly in the Cloud.

Copy.com is a new competitor of Dropbox, a promising "newcomer" among cloud data storages. Its functionality is almost identical to Dropbox. The developer of this service is Barracuda Networks company, the activity of which is data protection, good security and data protection is announced. The advantages of Copy.com include a beautiful and clear interface; cross-platform service - there are applications for Android, iOS, Linux, Mac OS X, Windows and Windows Phone; no limit on the size of the downloaded file.

Cloud computing architecture and models
Cloud Computing Architecture

Let's take a look at cloud computing and see what cloud computing consists of. Cloud computing consists of two components: frontend and backend (Fig. 5.1). The frontend consists of the client side of the cloud computing system. It consists of the interfaces and applications required to access the cloud computing platform.

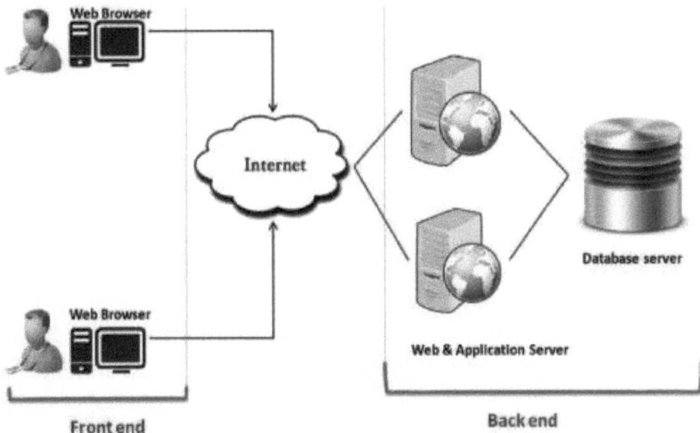

Figure 5.1. Composition of cloud computing

Each section has very specific meanings and spheres and is connected to the others through some kind of virtual network or network environment of the Internet.

UI refers to the part of cloud computing that is visible to its user, which is realised through a sequence of interfaces and applications that allow their consumer to perform access to the cloud system in question. Different cloud computing systems have different UIs (User Interface).

The internal partition is the part that is not visible to its user. This section contains all those resources that allow the provider to provide cloud computing services such as servers, storage and virtual machines. The basic idea behind the back-end is to entrust the necessary management of the entire system to a separate central server, which thus has a constantly monitored exchange and requests from users, managing access and implementing communication protocols.

Apart from the various components of this architecture, the most important is the Hypervisor, also called *Virtual Machine Manager*. This is the firmware that dynamically allocates resources and also allows you to share a single instance between multiple users. In short, it is the software that implements virtualisation, which is one of the main features of cloud computing.

Although the server part refers to the cloud itself, it includes the resources required for cloud computing services. It consists of virtual machines, servers, data storage, security mechanism, etc. It is under the control of the provider.

Cloud computing distributes a file system that is spread across multiple hard drives and machines. Data is never stored in only one place and in case of failure of one unit, another unit will automatically take possession. The user's disc space is allocated in the distributed file system, while the other important component is the algorithm for resource allocation.

Cloud computing is a strong distributed environment that is highly dependent on a strong algorithm.

Cloud Computing Component Levels

The following levels of cloud computing architecture are differentiated.

The client layer is the client *software* used to access cloud services, such as a *web browser.*

The service layer is the services themselves used through the cloud model.

The application layer is software that can be accessed via the cloud and does not require installation on the user's computer (as already mentioned, this is one of the main advantages of the cloud model).

The platform layer is a software platform that integrates a complete set of tools for deploying and using cloud computing on a user's computer (without additional installations, hardware purchases, etc.). An example of such a platform is **Microsoft.NET Azure Services Platform**.

Memory Layer - *support for* storing and accessing user data via the cloud. In fact, a set of *Web sites* implemented on data centre computers is used to store user data.

Infrastructure layer - providing a complete virtualised platform via the cloud, such as Amazon *Web* Services.

Cloud Computing Architecture

Let's consider a diagram of cloud computing architecture:

- **Services** available through the cloud
- **Infrastructure** for their deployment and use
- **Platform** - a set of tools for using the cloud
- **Memory** - support for storing user data in the data centre implementing the cloud
- **The cloud architect** is the principal designer of the **cloud** architecture.
- **A cloud integrator** is its system administrator who is responsible for

adding components to the cloud and modifying them.

Cloud components are typically *Web services*.

Fig. 5.2 shows an example of a typical cloud computing architecture.

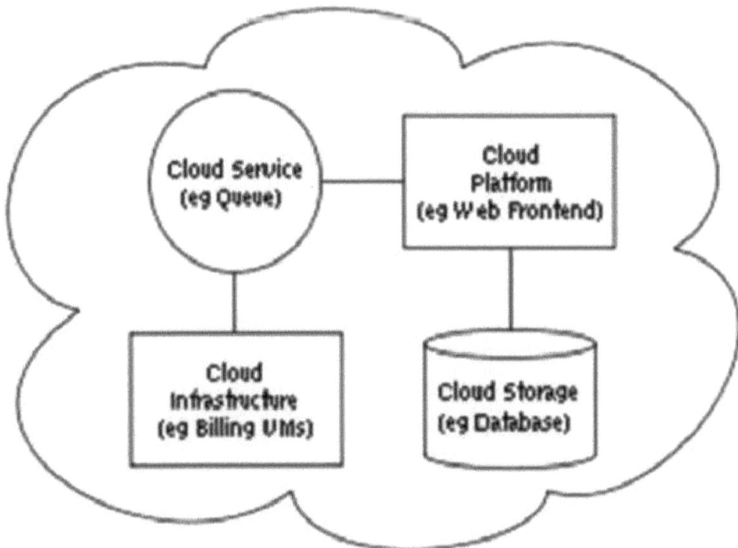

Figure 5.2. An example of a typical cloud computing architecture

The user directly accesses a *cloud service,* such as a *Queue* concept. *Access* to this service is part of the *cloud platform that* provides a *Web-frontend that is* convenient for accessing the service. As the *experience of* using the new version of *Windows* Azure shows, the modern cloud *Web-interface is* as convenient as the usual graphical user interface *of* local applications, so that the *user will* hardly feel any difference between them. Through the cloud platform is available *cloud storage* (in *Windows* Azure - *Storage* component), including - *database, for* example, in the Azure cloud is *SQL Server Azure.* Finally, through cloud services, *cloud infrastructure* (e.g. *virtual machines*) is available.

Roles in cloud computing

When using cloud computing, the roles of the professionals involved also change slightly compared to the use of traditional *software.*

The cloud provider is the data centre.

Cloud users can be any internet users.

A cloud **hardware or software vendor** is a company that provides hardware and underlying software development for a data centre.

In recent years, a new role has also emerged - participation in a **cloud**

community of professionals interested in cloud computing, such as the *IEEE Cloud Computing Community.*

Cloud computing standards

The cloud computing model is based on adherence to a number of *standards.* Standards are used for application interoperability:

* **HTTP** (basic Web protocol);
* **XMPP (Jabber)** is a standard for sending and receiving instant messages in XML format; the word *jabber* literally means "chatter"; interestingly, XML "phrases" in this protocol are called *stanzas (stanza)* in a poetic manner;

- **SSL** *(Secure Socket Layer)-a* layer of secure socket network connections used, for example, in the **https** protocol.

Web-browsers (with active use of **AJAX** *(Asynchronous JavaScript and XML)* technology, which allows to reduce the number of redirections from one web-page to another and, thus, significantly reduce the *waiting time* and access to the user to the information he needs) and offline-clients based on *HTML 5* (a special version of *HTML* for cloud computing) are used to work with clients in the cloud.

The principles of software and data virtualisation and the *OMF* standard are used to implement the cloud.

For interaction with services, data is transferred in *XML* format.

Cloud *Web-services, as* a rule, function on the basis of the standard *Representational State Transfer (REST)* - transfer of information about the state through arguments and results of *Web-methods*. This standard provides the greatest efficiency of their work.

The main service models in cloud systems

Cloud computing and the services it provides (e.g., computing power or storage) can be compared to utilities. Just as the consumption of water and electricity changes in hot or cold weather, the consumption of services provided by cloud platforms can increase or decrease depending on the increase or decrease of loads. The similarity between services and utilities lies in several aspects. First, in both, consumers only pay for the actual disposal. Second, both are leased resources - i.e., in most cases, one does not need to connect to a well for water or directly to a power plant for electricity - the providers of such services make them available as leased "resources," leaving the issues of building and maintaining infrastructure to themselves. Thirdly, by entering into a contract with a relevant organisation, the availability of these or those resources is implied, and the organisation - timely payment of their rent.

Currently, it is common to distinguish **three main cloud service models, which are sometimes referred to as cloud layers. It can be said that these three layers - infrastructure services, platform services and application services - reflect the structure not only of cloud technologies, but also of information technologies in general** (Fig. 5.3.). Let us elaborate on each of them.

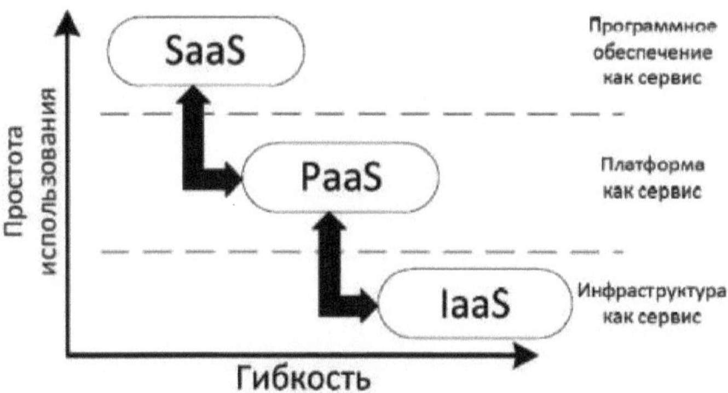

Figure 5.3. Main service models in cloud systems

Infrastructure as a Service. The *Infrastructure as a Service (IaaS)* model provides an opportunity to lease infrastructure resources such as servers, storage devices and network equipment. The entire infrastructure is managed by the service provider, and the consumer only manages the OS and installed applications. Such services are usually charged on a pay-as-you-go basis and allow the user to increase or decrease the amount of infrastructure used through special portals provided by the service providers. Here the consumers are application owners, IT specialists preparing OS images to run them on the service infrastructure. The cloud platform provides services to run virtual machines and storage services. The service-level agreement (*SLA*) usually covers service characteristics such as virtual server availability, OS image deployment time. Almost any application installed on standard OS images can be run in this service model. As with *PaaS*, infrastructure as a service is usually paid for based on the amount of resources used.

Infrastructure services address the challenge of properly equipping the data centre by providing computing capacity as needed. Typically, these services support infrastructure and a much larger number of consumers than application services. A particular example of infrastructure services is *Hardware as a Service (HaaS)*. As a service, the user receives hardware on the basis of which they deploy their own infrastructure using the most appropriate software.

The consumer does not control the underlying cloud infrastructure, but has control over operating systems, storage, deployed applications, and possibly limited control over the choice of network components (e.g., host with firewalls). In such a case, platform and application protection is provided by the consumer, and the cloud provider must organise infrastructure protection. Virtualisation is often used to provide resources on demand.

Benefits. Reduced hardware investment. As this model typically uses virtualisation techniques, savings can be made as a result of more efficient use of resources. Reduced risk of loss of investment and adoption threshold, and the ability to scale smoothly and automatically.

Disadvantages. Business efficiency and productivity are very dependent on the vendor's capabilities. There is a likelihood that potentially large long-term costs will be required. Centralisation requires new approaches to security measures.

Examples of infrastructure services include IBM SmartCloud Enterprise, VMWare, Amazon EC2, Windows Azure, Parallels Cloud Server, the Google Apps suite, which includes Google Mail, Google Docs Google and Cloud Storage, and many others.

Platform as a Service (*PaaS*). The *Platform as a Service (PaaS)* model provides the ability to rent a platform, which typically includes OS and application services. Platform as a Service facilitates the development, testing, deployment and maintenance of applications without the need to invest in infrastructure and software environment. Platform as a service also includes infrastructure as a service. Examples of Platform as a Service include *Windows Azure, Amazon Web Services* (*AWS*).

Here, the consumers are the companies that developed the applications themselves. The platform provides the application runtime environment, data storage services, and a number of additional services, such as integration or communication services. A service-level agreement (*SLA*) usually covers service characteristics such as the availability of the application runtime environment and its performance. The ability to customise applications to meet customer needs is virtually unlimited. Only the functionality of services provided at the platform level can be a limitation. However, it is important to realise that in order to take advantage of the cloud platform, existing applications need to be significantly upgraded or rewritten.

Cloud platform fees are calculated based on the amount of computing resources used, such as:

- application runtime;
- volume of data and number of data operations (transactions);

- network traffic.

The cloud platform provider may offer significant discounts when you purchase a certain amount of resources.

PaaS includes, among others, middleware as a service, messaging as a service, integration as a service, information as a service, communication as a service, etc. For example, ***Workplace as a Service (WaaS)*** allows a company to use cloud computing to organise the workplaces of its employees by configuring and installing all the software necessary for the staff to work. ***Data as a Service (DaaS)* provides users with disc space that** they can use to store large amounts of information. ***Security as a Service (SaaS)*** enables users to quickly deploy products that enable secure web usage, secure email, and secure local system security. This service allows users to save money on deploying and maintaining their own security system.

In other words, the PaaS model is IaaS with the operating system and its Application Programming Interface (API). The consumer does not control the underlying cloud infrastructure, including networks, servers, operating systems and storage, but has control over the deployed applications and possibly some configuration parameters of the hosting environment. Thus, the consumer must take care to ensure that the applications to be deployed on the provided platforms are protected.

Applications can run either in the cloud or in traditional enterprise data centres. To achieve the scalability required in the cloud, the various services offered are often virtualised, similar to the infrastructure services discussed earlier.

Benefits. Smooth version deployment. Smoothness means that ideally the user should have little or no perception of software changes in the cloud.

Disadvantages. As with the previous service model, centralisation requires robust security measures.

Examples of platform services include IBM SmartCloud Application Services, Amazon Web Services, Windows Azure, Boomi, Cast Iron, Google App Engine, and others.

Software as a Service (*SaaS*). Software as a Service - SaaS involves access to applications as a service, i.e. the provider's applications run in the cloud and are provided to users on demand as a service. In other words, the **user can access software deployed on remote servers via the Internet, and all issues of updates and licences for this software are regulated by the provider of this service.** Payment in this case is made for the actual use of the software. Sometimes these services are free of charge, as they have the opportunity to generate revenue, for example, from advertising.

The Software as a Service (*SaaS*) model provides the ability to rent applications. Software as a Service includes Platform as a Service and Infrastructure as a Service. An example of an application as a service is *Business Productivity Online Suite*. The Software as a Service model is a model of providing access to applications via the Internet with payment for their use. This model is the most common cloud service delivery model today. Organisations can implement such a service delivery model from private clouds using internal network channels, additionally secured and unconnected to the Internet. The consumers of this type of service are the end users who run the applications provided in the cloud. A service-level agreement (*SLA*) usually covers service characteristics such as *uptime* and performance. There is little or no customisation of applications to meet the needs of consumers, and the level of customisation is dictated by market requirements or the capabilities of the application providers. Payment for the final service is usually made on a monthly basis and is calculated based on the number of users of the application.

Applications are accessed through various client devices or through thin client interfaces, such as, for example, web browser, or webmail, or programme interfaces. The consumer does not manage the underlying infrastructure of the cloud, including networks, servers, operating systems. The end user is only responsible for the security of access parameters (logins, passwords, etc.) and for following the provider's recommendations for secure application settings.

Application services are most familiar to the everyday user. The most common examples of applications of this type are the mail services GMail, Mail.ru, Yahoo Mail. In general, there are thousands of SaaS applications, and thanks to Web 2.0 technology, their number is growing every day. Among application services there are many applications aimed at the corporate community. There is software that manages payroll, human resources, teamwork, relationships with customers and business partners, etc.

Benefits. Reduced capital investment in hardware and labour; reduced risk of investment loss; smooth iterative upgrades.

From the user's point of view, the ***main advantage of SaaS*** is its ***price advantage over "classic" software***. SaaS is paid on a pay-as-you-use model, which means that there is no need to invest in your own hardware and software infrastructure.

Disadvantages. As with the previous two models, centralisation requires robust security measures.

Examples of SaaS include Amazon's cloud, Amazon Web Services, consisting of Elastic Compute Cloud (EC2), which provides information resources as services, Simple Storage Service (S3) for information storage, Gmail, Google Docs, Netflix, Photoshop.com, Acrobat.com, Intuit QuickBooks Online, IBM LotusLive, Unyte, Salesforce.com, Sugar CRM, and WebEx. A significant portion of the growing mobile application market is also SaaS implementations.

Other service models in cloud systems

▶ **Hardware as a Service (HaaS): the** user is provided with equipment on a lease basis which he can use for his own purposes. In essence, HaaS is similar to IaaS, except that you have bare hardware on the basis of which you deploy your own infrastructure using the most appropriate software. The advantage of HaaS is the ability to save on equipment maintenance.

▶ **Workplace as a Service (WaaS): a** company uses cloud computing to organise the workplaces of its employees by configuring and installing all the necessary software required for staff work.

▶ **Data as a Service (DaaS): the** user is provided with disc space that can be used to store large amounts of information.

▶ **Security as a Service:** users can quickly deploy products that enable secure use of web, email, and local systems, saving them the cost of maintaining their own security.

▶ **Everything as a Service (EaaS): Everything** from hardware and software to business process management, including user-to-user interaction, will be provided to the user with Internet access. EaaS is just a more general concept in relation to the above services.

It is believed that the currently accepted division of cloud computing will become a thing of the past in the near future as technology evolves. Cloud applications of the future are expected to combine not only infrastructure and platform elements from a single vendor, but also different services from different vendors. Perhaps cloud computing will eventually lead to the concept of **Everything as a Service (EaaS)**. In this type of service, the user will be provided with everything from hardware and software to business process management, including interaction between users.

Architecture and features of cloud file systems

A distributed file system for cloud is a file system with a distributed architecture that provides users with simultaneous full network access to data/files.

Objectives:

▶ optimisation of batch data processing (e.g. with MapReduce);

▶ *high availability,* access to data when system nodes may fail;

▶ support for complex system topology (geographically separated nodes and clusters);

▶ support for large files (up to several TB) and a large number of files;

▶ Using TCP/IP and remote procedure calls to access data.

Characteristics of cloud-based FSs:

▶ splitting files into blocks (~ a few MB) to optimise access;

▶ duplication of blocks on multiple nodes for fault tolerance. Often geographically separated nodes are selected to optimise access speed.

▶ dedicated servers for storing metadata (block matches to files, file positions in directories, ...).

Examples of cloud-based FSs:

▶ Google File System;

▶ Hadoop Distibuted File System (HDFS);

▶ Lustre;

▶ IBM General Parallel File System (GPFS).

Architecture of cloud file systems

A typical architecture of cloud file systems is shown in Fig. 6.1.

Figure 6.1. Typical architecture of cloud file systems

The growing popularity of cloud technologies has caused a surge of new requirements for file systems (FS). A new type of file system is emerging that uses cloud storage as a backend interface.

Such file systems are used to utilise one or more cloud resources and solve some of the limitations such as data storage security, availability, access latency. At the same time, clients can access data stored in cloud file systems both via SMB/NFS protocols and by mounting them as local file systems.

The most important step towards the adaptation of such solutions was the emergence of a single interface - CDMI (*Cloud Data Management* Interface), which is a unified standard of REST ful HTTP operations that will be used to create, update, delete and request objects from the cloud. It will also be used by management applications to edit container metadata (Fig. 6.2).

File systems translate requests to them into CDMI requests and have caching capabilities to provide fast access to objects.

Some cloud file systems also provide additional features such as client-side data compression and encryption.

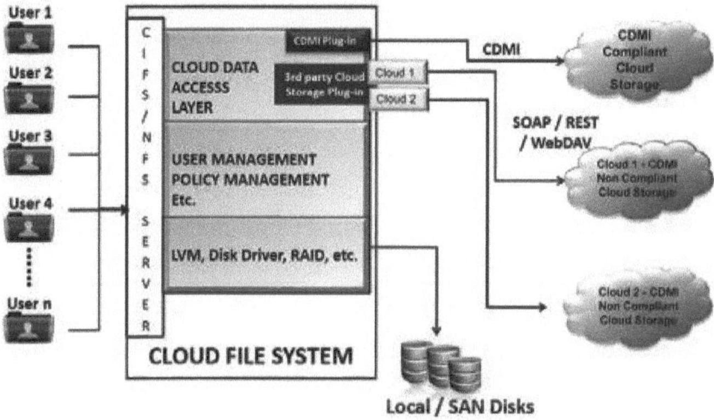

Figure 6.2. Architecture of cloud file systems

Until recently, there was only one public standard related to file system operation.

POSIX *(*Portable *Operating System Interface*), which describes the operation of UNIX-like operating systems, came from IEEE 1003.1_1988, developed back in 1988. The last change to POSIX file system IO was made in 1991.

With the emergence of the web, the need for a new interface became obvious, as it was impossible to make a system call via HTTP. At the turn of the millennium, one of the founders of the HTTP protocol described REST (*Representational State Transfer*).

In the last 3 years with the migration of applications and storage to the cloud, the popularity of the REST interface has grown tremendously. It is believed that REST will eventually replace POSIX for all types of applications.

POSIX has been a major standard for 35 years - there are millions of applications that support it. At the same time, it has not been changed in over 20 years. There have been many proposals to improve it, but they require extensive testing and updates to operating system stacks, which is not supported by many of the vendors that are members of the OpenGroup, which oversees POSIX development.

Ensuring metadata correctness when multiple threads competitively access the same data is quite challenging for parallel file systems storing billions of files and applications that may require many parallel I/O operations.

POSIX allows you to read or write a portion of a file, which REST does not.

Among the major POSIX issues are the structure of file discriptors (inodes) and the requirements for atomicity of operations.

REST uses a small set of predefined methods to access objects.

The main advantage of REST is its flexibility: the developer of the control system can create any new special methods within certain boundaries.

One of today's challenges, as discussed earlier, is the ability to create file systems that support storing billions of objects in a single namespace. There are, however, few POSIX-compliant systems that scale to 10 petabytes of data and billions of objects. Not all of them support competitive accesses to a single file (for example, this is a limitation of GlusterFS).

On the other hand, if the objects are very large, we cannot perform reads on them until the move operation is completed using the REST interface.

REST and SOAP (*SOAP-Simple Object Access Protocol*) interfaces will not be able to be applied to applications requiring asynchronous access and random positioning within a file, but on infrastructures requiring a high degree of scalability, POSIX has a strong competitor.

File systems used in private and hybrid clouds have additional requirements that cannot be met by standard parallel distributed file systems.

One of the challenges of distributed file systems is to ensure the protection of client data. Cloud file systems require isolation of file system namespaces for different users, encryption at the file system level on the user side, UID/GUID isolation (***UID* - Unique** user identifier, ***GUID*** (Globally Unique Identifier) - statistically unique 128-bit identifier) to prevent conflicts, quota enforcement and finally usage control for billing tasks (Billing system - application software to support billing business processes).

Oracle introduced Oracle Cloud File System in 2011. The main goal of the development was to significantly reduce the cost and complexity of managing storage infrastructure in private clouds.

Oracle Cloud File System allows you to:

- deploy a shared pool of storage resources with a single namespace for applications, operating files, and user files;
- provide access to stored data over the storage network or over conventional networks;
- rapidly increase, decrease, and migrate storage resources without stopping applications.

OSFS is based on the ASM product well known to Oracle DBMS administrators (Fig. 6.3).

Oracle Cloud File System uses Automatic Storage Management Dynamic Volume Manager (ADVM) as the volume management service for ASM Cluster File System and other file systems.

ADVM, designed for use in single-node and cluster environments, has ASM features such as dynamic space allocation, is cross-platform, and is easily managed through ASM CMD, EM, and SQL.

Oracle Automatic Storage Management Cluster File System is a general-purpose, high-availability cache-coherent cluster file system for storing any type of file.

ACFS (ASM Cluster File System) is a POSIX, X/OPEN, and Windows compatible file system.

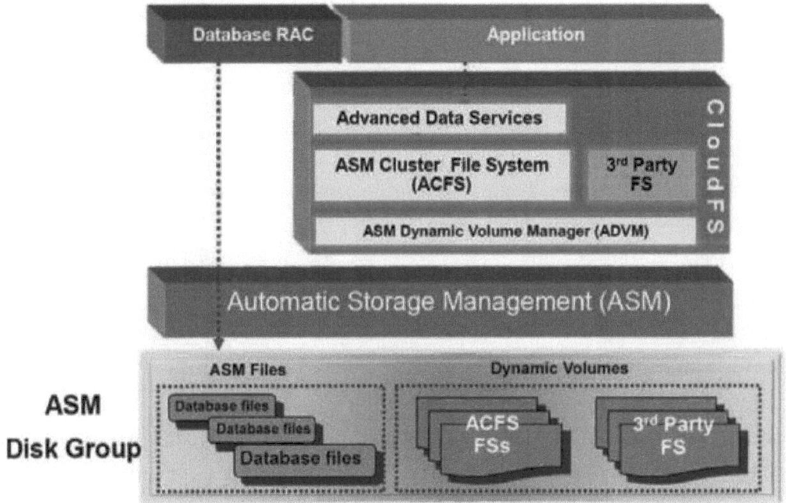

Figure 6.3. High-level architecture of Oracle Cloud File System.

ACFS can be used in both single-node and cluster infrastructures and has the following functionality:
- *snapshots* performed using copy_on_write technology. On-demand file recovery is provided;

- *tagging*, which allows the user to group multiple files together and perform group actions on them;
- *active-standby replication* to provide a disaster-resistant solution. Replication is accomplished by asynchronous transfer and playback of log files to the secondary site;
- *advanced security tools that* run on top of operating system tools. ACFS System Security allows users to create security realms, defines user and group security policies, and provides access control to file system objects.

The security domain of ACFS System Security is a virtual container of files and directories. Access rights to the container are defined by a security filter consisting of access rules and rule sets, as well as operation execution rights.

The ACFS security system is only managed by applying a special security administrator password other than the primary administrator password;
- *Encryption is* another mechanism to protect information in the cloud from unauthorised access.

ACFS System Encryption allows users to encrypt data located on storage (storage system) and provides keys for decryption. You can encrypt the entire file system as well as individual folders and files.

Cloud file storage

Cloud storage is a cloud computing model that involves storing data on the Internet using a cloud computing resource provider that provides and manages data storage as a service. Cloud storage is provided on-demand in the amount required, is pay-as-you-go, and eliminates the need to purchase and manage your own storage infrastructure. This provides flexibility, global scalability and reliability. Data is available anytime, anywhere.

Cloud file storage is a way to store files in the cloud, allowing servers and applications to access data through shared file systems. This compatibility makes cloud file storage ideal for workloads with shared file systems, and provides easy integration without code changes.

What is a cloud file system?

A file system in the cloud is a hierarchical storage system that provides shared access to file data. It allows you to create, delete, modify, read and write files, and organise them logically in a tree-like directory system for intuitive access.

What is file sharing in the cloud?

Cloud file sharing can be described as a service that provides multiple users with simultaneous access to a common set of file data in the cloud. The security of cloud file sharing is determined by permissions for individual users and groups, allowing administrators to strictly control access to shared file data.

What is cloud storage used for?

- For storing massive data, such as CCTV footage.
- As content repositories, such as public databases, distance education schools or multimedia resources.
- For storing Big Data, Internet of Things and machine learning data sets.
- Large media outlets are integrating clouds into their content supply chains, for example for archiving or storage for later analytics.
- To store data from gaming platforms like Google Stadia.
- Video hosting or photostocks use storage to stream content.
- As hosting for online shops, portals, blogs and other static sites.
- For microservices : cloud storage supports containerisation, process isolation and shared access.

But five scenarios are more common.

5 cloud storage scenarios:

№1. Backup and Restore.

№2. Software development and testing.

№3. Sharing.

№4. Data migration to the cloud

№5. Big Data and IoT.

Backup and recovery. Most cloud file systems are compatible with databases, so storage is often used for backups, such as for upgrades. Backup in the cloud is easier to set up, with better storage reliability because the service provider distributes copies to data centres.

Software development and testing. Often development requires duplication of environments, which then need to be removed, and collaboration. Using cloud resources for this is standard practice among software developers. Also, clouds integrate with different applications without additional "crutches".

Shared access. For example, for development and testing teams from different offices or cities. If data is stored on a server within the enterprise network, a VPN is often required. But you can do without it and move some of the shared files, which are usually the ones you need access to, to cloud storage.

Migrating data to the cloud makes it easier to maintain your infrastructure, but it's a major task that requires years of experience from a system administrator. However, there are services that make the process easier.

Big Data and IoT. For example, for Big Data, a 100 Terabyte data set is not that much, but it is expensive to keep such a volume on local servers, so clouds are often used for this purpose. It is convenient to store arrays in the cloud: cloud services usually have high bandwidth, low latency, and the ability to customise queries without retrieving data.

How does cloud storage work?

Cloud storage is purchased from a third-party cloud service provider that owns, manages and provides access to data storage resources over the Internet on a pay-as-you-use basis. Cloud storage providers are responsible for resource health, security and reliability, ensuring data availability for customer applications worldwide.

Applications access cloud storage through traditional storage protocols or directly through APIs. Many vendors offer additional services designed to protect, collect, analyse and manage data on a massive scale.

Benefits of cloud storage

There are two parties in the model: the client and the service provider. The client rents space on the provider's servers and stores documents, applications, static content of websites on them, accessing them remotely. The provider organises storage, maintenance, security and access to the data.

Storing data in the cloud allows IT departments to fundamentally rethink three aspects of their operations.

1. **Total cost of ownership.** With cloud storage, you don't need to purchase hardware, allocate storage resources, or spend cash for something that "might come in handy someday." You can add or remove resources on demand, quickly change performance and retention periods. And in doing so, you'll only pay for the resources you use. Data that isn't used as often can be automatically moved to more cost-effective tiers by rules that are easy to control. This allows you to deliver savings at high volumes.

For your own storage system you will need: space, racks, servers, cooling, infrastructure equipment. Backups will need to be organised with the purchase of software and additional storage devices. And all of this will need to be maintained by administrators, such as periodic preventive maintenance with shutdowns and upgrades.

With cloud storage, most operational costs are reduced and capital costs are eliminated.

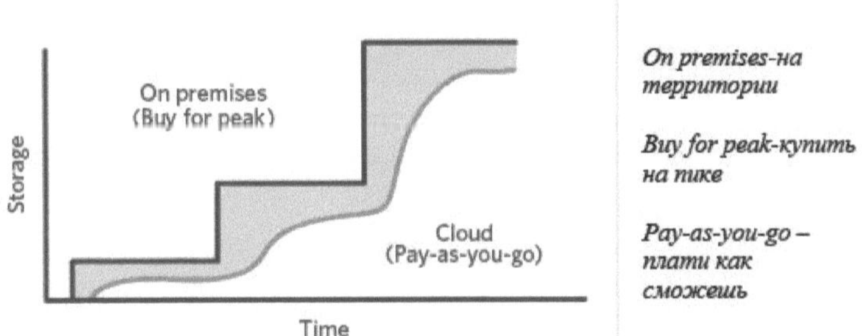

Figure 6.4. Efficiency of cloud technology

2. **Time to deployment.** When development teams are ready to launch projects, infrastructure doesn't have to hold them back. Cloud storage allows IT to quickly allocate the necessary storage space exactly when it's needed. As a result, IT can focus on solving complex application problems rather than on storage management issues.

3. **Information management.** Centralised storage in the cloud creates tremendous opportunities for new use cases. Using lifecycle management policies in cloud storage, you can address important information management challenges, including automatic tiering or locking down data for compliance purposes.

Cloud storage requirements

Ensuring the reliable storage, security and availability of critical enterprise data is of paramount importance. There are several fundamental requirements when considering cloud storage.

A good cloud file storage solution should provide the performance and bandwidth to meet your current challenges and the ability to scale efficiently as your business needs change.

Full control

Provides a fully managed file system that can be up and running in minutes.

Performance

Provides stable bandwidth and low-latency performance

Compatibility

Integrates efficiently with existing applications without the need to create programming code

Reliability. Data should be stored with redundancy. Ideally, they should be distributed across multiple sites and multiple devices within each site. Natural disasters, human error or mechanical failures should not result in data loss.

Cloud storage is maintained by engineers with specialised experience in operating this type of system.

ISP administrators regularly upgrade hardware, improve software, and work on security.

In this case, the data is stored "with a reserve": the supplier reserves 2 GB for storing 1 GB of client data. Servers are often distributed across several cities or countries, which adds **fault tolerance in** case of force majeure.

Accessibility. All data should be accessible when needed, but there is a difference between production data and archives. The ideal cloud storage offers the best combination between data retrieval time and cost. Data can be managed via GUIs, console or APIs.

Availability when you need it by redundant copying across multiple locations

Security. Ideally, all data should be encrypted - both in storage and in transmission. Permissions and access controls should work the same way in the cloud as they do in local data storage.

There are two aspects here: physical and data transmission security.

•   The first aspect is ensured by the fact that a data centre is usually a secure, 24/7 building with video surveillance, access control and accounting systems. Inside there are cooling, fire-fighting and backup power supply systems, which are duplicated for reliability.

•   The second is account access rights settings, monitoring, encryption during downloading, reading and storing data. Not including additional security vendor services.

Scaling. The capacity is quickly increased by connecting additional servers and storage. It's also fast in the physical version, but only if you take care of scaling in advance. And it's also going to be expensive and **"vendor lock-in"**. This means that you will be tied to the vendor and its platform, technology, software. When you want to change vendors, you will have to build everything anew, because all hardware and software is tied to the vendor.

Cost management. You should pay exactly as much as you consume resources. Object stores have classes - standard, "cold", "ice". Classes help to manage storage costs. For example, when data needs to be accessed frequently, you can pay more for storage, but cheaper for traffic (accesses). For archives, the opposite is true - you can pay more for working with files, but cheaper for storage, because they are rarely accessed.

Business processes are simplified when cloud storage is available to an employee, for example, from home on weekends. And let's not forget about **data recovery,** when business processes are not interrupted by force majeure due to loss of documents or repository.

Examples of cloud file storage use cases

Cloud file storage is ideal for workloads such as large content repositories, development environments, media repositories and user home directories.

Cloud file storage solutions are flexible, integrate seamlessly with existing applications, are easy to deploy and maintain, and are easy to manage. This makes it possible to support a wide range of applications at different levels.

Distribution of files via the Internet

The need for shared file storage for applications that distribute files over the Internet can lead to difficulties in integrating the server parts of the applications. Typically, there are multiple web servers delivering website content, with each web server needing access to the same set of files. Because cloud file storage solutions support traditional file system semantics, file naming conventions, and permissions familiar to web developers, such storage can easily provide the integration of the required Internet applications.

Content management

A content management system (CMS) (Content - Information) requires a common namespace and access to a file system hierarchy. As in the example of distributing files over the Internet, CMS environments typically have multiple servers that need access to the same set of files to serve content. Because cloud file storage solutions support traditional file system semantics, file naming conventions, and the permissions familiar to web developers, these repositories of documents and other files can be easily integrated into existing CMS workflows.

Big data analytics

Big data requires storage that can handle very large amounts of data and scale as needs grow, as well as provide the performance needed to deliver the data to analytics tools. Many analytics workloads need a file interface to interact with the data and the ability to write to different parts of the file. In addition, these workflows often use standard file semantics such as locking. Because cloud file storage supports the necessary file system semantics and allows for scalable resources and performance, it is ideal for file sharing solutions that can be easily integrated into existing big data workflows.

Media and entertainment industry

Workflows in the digital media and entertainment industry are constantly changing. Many use hybrid cloud deployments and require standardised access using network file protocols such as NFS. These workflows require flexible, stable and secure access to data from both off-the-shelf and custom-built or partner solutions. Because cloud file storage supports traditional file system semantics, multimedia content storage for processing and collaboration can be easily integrated into digital media supply chains, content creation, media streaming, broadcast, analytics and archiving workflows.

Home catalogues

Using home directories for file storage that are only accessible to specific users and groups is optimal for many cloud-based workflows. Companies that expect to take advantage of the scalability and economics of the cloud are extending access to home directories to many of their users. Because cloud file storage solutions support traditional file system semantics and standard permission models, customers can easily migrate applications that require these capabilities to the cloud.

Database backup

Backing up data using existing mechanisms, software and semantics can be used to create an isolated recovery scenario with little location flexibility. Many companies are looking to utilise the flexibility of cloud storage for database backups as temporary protection during upgrades or to address development and testing issues. Because cloud file storage solutions provide a standard file system that can be simply plugged into database servers, they can be an ideal platform for creating portable database backups using in-built tools or enterprise backup applications.

Development tools

As you work together to develop innovative solutions in development environments, challenges can arise in sharing data securely and reliably. When software code and other files need to be shared, cloud file storage provides a streamlined and secure repository that can be easily accessed from within cloud development environments. Cloud file storage provides a scalable and highly available solution ideal for collaboration.

Storage for containers and serverless applications

Containers are ideal for creating microservices because they are simple to allocate and move, while providing the necessary process isolation. Containers that need access to source data on every run may require a shared file system with the ability to connect from any instance in use. Cloud file storage can provide continuous shared data access for all containers in the cluster. Using serverless computing, you can be more flexible in your operations while taking the time to ensure application security, scalability, and availability. AWS Lambda enables you to run large-scale and mission-critical serverless applications. Cloud file storage offers highly available and reliable serverless storage for sharing data that needs to be stored after and between AWS Lambda functions and AWS Fargate tasks.

Types of cloud storage

It is impractical to store Big Data and corporate document archives together. Each task requires a different type of cloud storage: object, block or file storage.

There are three types of cloud storage: object storage, file storage, and block storage. Each offers different benefits suitable for certain use cases.

1. **Object storage**. Applications developed in the cloud typically take advantage of the benefits of object storage, such as extensive scalability and storing object properties as metadata. Object storage, such as Amazon Simple Storage Service (S3), is ideal for developing from scratch modern applications that require flexibility and scalability. They can also be used to import data from existing storage for analytics, backup, or archiving purposes.

2. **File storage**. Some applications require access to shared files, hence the need for a file system. This type of storage is often supported by a network-attached storage (NAS) server. File storage solutions, such as Amazon Elastic File System (EFS), are ideal for use cases such as large content repositories, development environments, multimedia storage, or users' personal directories.

3. **Block storage.** Other enterprise applications,

For example, databases or enterprise resource planning systems (ERP), often require dedicated, low-latency storage for each of the nodes. Such storage works similarly to direct-attached storage (DAS) or a storage area network (SAN). Block-based cloud storage solutions, such as Amazon Elastic Block Store (EBS), allocate storage for each virtual server and provide ultra-low latency for performance-intensive workloads.

What is Block Storage?

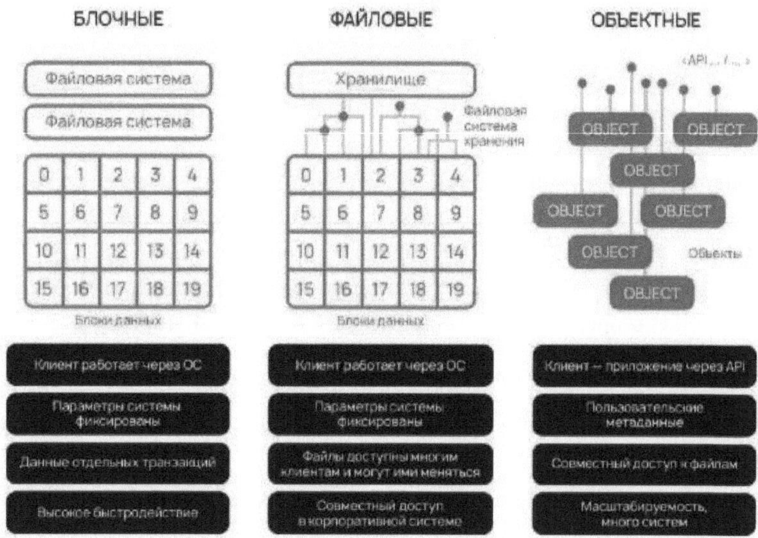

Figure 6.5. Types of cloud storage

In this type, files are divided into identical parts - chunks. Each chunk has its own location ID, which is used by the storage system to quickly reassemble the chunks back into files.

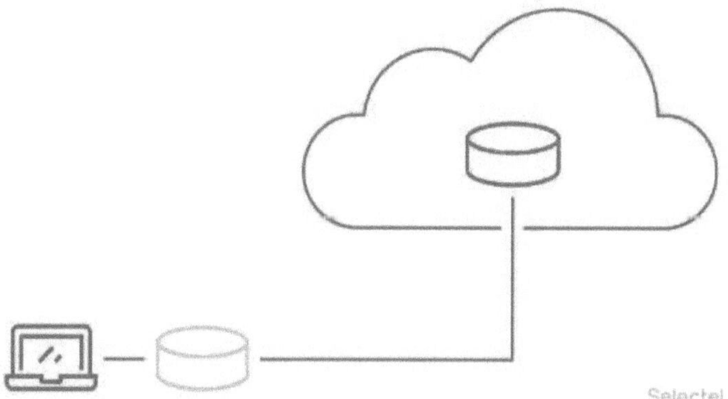

Fig. 6.6. Functioning principle of block storage

Benefits. With block storage, data user environments are separated. This allows you to distribute data across multiple environments and give separate access to them.

Low latency. All operating systems see block storage as disks and can connect to them via Fiber Channel or iSCSI (iSCSI - Internet Small

Computer System Interface), a **TCP/IP-based protocol designed for interconnecting and managing storage systems, servers and clients**.

How it's used. Often integrated with enterprise databases. Oracle, for example, use blockchain systems

- When data input/output (IO) speed and low latency (over SAN), are critical.
- When the amount of data is unknown in advance. Instead of a hard disc, a block storage is connected to the server so that the DBMS writes data to it. When the space runs out - more space is purchased and the database server increases its capacity without moving and adjustments.

Disadvantages. Lack of metadata limits data management. Additional information about blocks loads the database. Even without it, setting up block storage creates extra work: file system selection, permissions, version control, backups.

Also, this type is one of the most expensive because you have to pay for the entire dedicated space, even if it's empty.

What is File Storage?

The organisation of storage in file storage is familiar:

- information is stored in files;
- the files in the folders;
- and folders are combined into subfolders and directories.

Storage is organised hierarchically. To find a file, you need to know the full path: to the catalogue, subdirectory, folder and to the file. Both servers and PCs can access the file storage.

Advantages. Data is organised in a hierarchical directory tree, as in other operating systems such as Windows, and working with files is intuitive. Files are uploaded to the cloud via the web interface or a separate local folder.

How used. To work together (and simultaneously) because:

- easy to navigate;
- administrator can configure access and permissions to files and trees.

File storage systems are suitable for large amounts of structured data. For example, for companies that develop software or analyse data, where multiple servers are required to access and modify multiple files simultaneously.

Disadvantages. This type of storage does not scale well. As the amount of data grows, the hierarchy and permissions become so complex that they become difficult to navigate and the system itself slows down. Therefore, this type is rarely used in data centres.

What is cloud object storage?

Cloud object storage allows you to store virtually infinite amounts of data in its original format.

As businesses grow, they have to manage ever-growing but isolated pools of data from multiple sources and used in any number of applications and business processes. Many companies are now having trouble maintaining a set of separate silos that complicate operations and slow the development of business applications. Object Storage solves these problems by providing a scalable, wide-ranging and affordable data store of any type of data in source format.

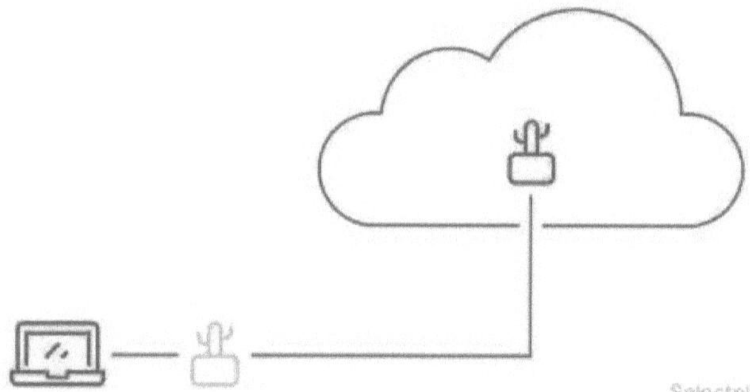

Fig. 6.7. Functioning principle of object storage

Object storage solutions on AWS (Amazon Web Services), such as Amazon Simple Storage Service (Amazon S3) and Amazon Glacier, allow you to manage storage in a centralised and easy-to-use application interface. Policies allow you to optimise the cost of storage and automatically switch between usage tiers based on the storage classes in use. AWS makes it easy to work with storage to perform analyses and derive valuable insights, allowing you to make decisions faster.

A relatively new and versatile way to store data. Suitable for any data: logs, accounting records, films, presentations, photos, programmes or static websites.

Versatility is achieved by storing files as objects with a set of properties. Properties store an identifier and metadata.

• An identifier (one) is a 128-bit number. Usually called universally (UUID) or globally (GUID) unique identifier.

• Metadata: name, coordinates, size, author name, and other information to identify the object.

Benefits of cloud object storage

There are three key benefits to storing data in the AWS object storage cloud service.

1. Reliability, availability, and scalability. Amazon S3 and Amazon Glacier are designed from the ground up for 99.999999999% reliability. Data is automatically distributed to a minimum of three physical data centres that are geographically separated by at least 10 kilometres within an AWS region. In addition, data can be automatically replicated to any other AWS region. According to Gartner, Inc. information, "Amazon S3 is the largest public cloud object storage service in terms of the amount of data served. Compared to any other vendor, AWS can provide more analytics on how customers use public cloud storage services at appropriate scale."

2. Security and compliance. Amazon S3 and Amazon Glacier are the only cloud storage services that support three different forms of encryption. AWS CloudTrail provides monitoring and logging of API calls. Amazon Macie provides a security service with artificial intelligence that performs continuous monitoring of data usage to detect anomalies and take timely action to prevent data loss or accidental publication. Amazon S3 and Glacier support more security standards and compliance certifications than any other service, including PCI-DSS, HIPAA/HITECH, FedRAMP, SEC Rule 17-a-4, EU Data Protection Directive, FISMA, and many others. This ensures compliance with the security requirements of virtually every regulatory agency in the world.

3. Management flexibility. AWS offers the most flexible set of options for storage management and administration. Storage administrators can categorise, visualise and report on data usage trends to reduce costs and improve service levels. Objects can be tagged with unique customisable metadata so customers can see and monitor storage usage, costs and security separately for each workload. The S3 Inventory tool generates scheduled reports about objects and their metadata for maintenance, compliance, and analytics. In addition, Amazon S3 can analyse object access patterns to create lifecycle policies that automate tiered storage, deletion and retention of data. Finally, because Amazon S3 is compatible with AWS Lambda, customers can log actions, define alerts, and invoke workflows - all without managing any additional infrastructure. Only AWS provides such a broad set of in-built management capabilities.

4. Data queries without extraction. Amazon S3 is the only cloud storage platform that allows you to perform sophisticated analyses on big data without having to extract it and move it to a separate analytics system. Anyone who knows SQL can use Amazon Athena to analyse on-demand massive amounts of unstructured data in Amazon S3. Using Amazon

Redshift Spectrum, customers can perform sophisticated analyses on exabytes of data in S3 and run queries that span data stored in both S3 and Redshift data stores.

5. Huge community. In addition to integration with most AWS services, the Amazon S3 and Amazon Glacier partner community includes tens of thousands of consulting companies, systems integrators, and independent software vendors. And new partners are joining every month. The AWS Marketplace offers 35 categories that cover more than 3,500 software products preconfigured for deployment in the AWS cloud from more than 1,100 independent software vendors. This means customers can easily use S3 and Glacier alongside popular backup, recovery and archiving solutions, the best big data solutions, innovative disaster recovery solutions and the latest on-premises primary storage environments. No other cloud provider has as many partners offering solutions pre-integrated to work with Object Storage Services.

Thanks to identifiers, the structure is flat - there is no hierarchy, which allows scaling up to hundreds of Petabytes. At the same time, metadata can be customised to meet specific application requirements: refine, rewrite, extend.

It is convenient for applications to access the data - parallel access via HTTP and S3 protocols is supported. All this is quite safe - modern object storage has a high level of reliability and low specific storage cost.

Examples of cloud object storage use cases

Backup and restore

Amazon S3 offers scalable and secure cloud storage with a high degree of reliability, which is great for backing up and archiving critical data. To further protect your data, you can use S3's version control feature. You can also define data lifecycle management rules to automatically migrate less frequently used data to standard S3 infrequent access storage and archive object sets to Amazon Glacier.

Benefits of backing up to the AWS cloud

Reliability of data storage

Backup protection with 99.999999999 % reliability. Copies of all data sent to Amazon S3 and Amazon S3 Glacier are created and stored on at least three devices in the same AWS region. Even when following the recommendations, local storage cannot match AWS in reliability, because AWS is all about global reach and security.

Flexibility and scalability

You can scale your backup resources in minutes as your data requirements change. With AWS, you no longer have to wait weeks or months to acquire tape media, discs and other IT resources to expand your storage infrastructure. On-demand scalability increases operational flexibility, pace of innovation and agility.

Cost-effectiveness

Pay-as-you-go, cost management tools, data lifecycle policies and multiple classes of EFS and S3 storage, including EFS Infrequent Access, S3 Standard-Infrequent Access, S3 One Zone-Infrequent Access, S3 Glacier and S3 Glacier Deep Archive, combine to create a cost-effective solution. These features help you protect your data in the cloud cost-effectively and without sacrificing performance. Sending backups to AWS can be the first step in reducing the TCO and costs of your data centre.

Backup of all types of data

AWS allows you to back up all types of data. Our storage services for objects (Amazon S3 and Amazon S3 Glacier), files (Amazon Elastic File System), and blocks (Amazon Elastic Block Storage) deliver industry-leading scalability, availability, reliability, and security. Your backups are secure and available when you need them.

Safety and compliance

Protect your backups with network architecture and data centres that were originally designed for organisations with high security requirements. Manage access, monitor atypical activity, encrypt data, and audit with <u>AWS security services</u>. AWS also supports <u>compliance programmes to </u>help customers meet all regulatory requirements.

Data transfer methods

Interoperating with AWS will allow you to optimise data transfers over the Internet (Amazon Direct Connect and S3 Transfer Acceleration), move petabytes and exabytes of data offline (AWS Snowball, AWS Snowmobile and AWS Snowball Edge), and deploy AWS Storage Gateway to connect local operations to AWS.

Data archiving and compliance

Amazon S3 and Amazon Glacier provide several classes of vaults to meet the needs of both organisations in regulated industries that need to store archives to meet regulatory requirements, and organisations that need active archives with the ability to access archived data quickly and infrequently. Amazon Glacier Vault Lock provides single write and multiple read (WORM) vaulting to meet records retention requirements. Lifecycle Policies simplify the process of moving data from Amazon S3 to <u>Amazon Glacier </u>by helping to automate the data migration process with specially defined policies.

Benefits of archiving in AWS

Cloud storage at the lowest prices

Prices for AWS archive storage solutions start at about $1 USD per terabyte per month. They are less expensive than the on-premises tape infrastructure used by customers.

Ensuring compliance with regulatory requirements

Customer compliance is critical, so AWS initiates regular third-party audits of thousands of global requirements that we monitor on an ongoing basis to help you meet security and regulatory standards in virtually any area.

Business flexibility

Quickly move data from archives to production environments in milliseconds, whenever you need it, and extract analytics with easy access to related AWS services. Customers can extend cloud workflows both rapidly and incrementally, or deploy new business models that leverage resource archives.

No hardware management is required

Simplify data archiving and eliminate the complexity of managing local tape drive libraries or secondary storage services by easily replacing your tape drive infrastructure without changing existing backups or archiving workflows.

Data protection and integrity

Data stored in AWS archiving solutions is highly available, 99.999999999% stable, and securely protected from corruption and damage for decades. Data stored in AWS archiving solutions can be made immutable. This provides an additional layer of data protection that prevents malicious or accidental deletion or modification of records, even with access rights.

Unlimited scaling with pay-as-you-go pricing

Ensure you're always meeting the unpredictable bandwidth demands of exponential data growth, and pay only for what you use, without a large upfront capital investment.

How they use it.

- To store large data sets, such as backup logs.
- For backups, archiving, for example, video recordings of a video production studio over 10 years.
- For storing and distributing mobile and web application content: images, images, software updates. For example, S3-enabled object stores can use plug-ins, extensions and libraries, and CDNs to accelerate the distribution of updates.
- E-commerce to store static content of online shops, for example.

Disadvantages. The 128-bit identifier adds complexity to object naming. For example, this is why Digital Asset Managers (DAM) exists as software that overlays an organisational chart on top of the object store. Such additional software would have to be used for companies that produce, for example, video content.

Another disadvantage is that you cannot write a file to object storage by dragging it from folder to folder. A programme interface - API - is used for interaction.

Conclusion: the main advantage of cloud storage

This is a reduction in operational costs. "Homemade" solutions (both cheap and expensive) need to be administered, backed up, updated when vulnerabilities are released. This is a separate job that should be handled by a separate person. Keeping a system administrator for this in the long run is sometimes more expensive than buying all the equipment (capital expenditure) for storage. The cloud is an alternative to in-house storage for storage in the corporate system, which removes a large layer of problems and operational costs.

Analysing big data

Amazon S3 can be used as a data lake to analyse big data for any application, from storing medical and financial records to multimedia data such as photos and videos. The Amazon Web Services suite contains everything you need to work with big data, reduce costs, scale, and grow fast. Amazon S3 is the only cloud storage service that allows you to query data without retrieval, eliminating expensive and time-consuming data extraction, transformation and loading (ETL) processes.

AWS provides the widest range of analytics services to meet your data analytics needs and enable organisations of all sizes and across multiple disciplines to re-create business with data. Data movement and storage, big data analytics, data lakes and machine learning (ML), log and streaming data analytics, business intelligence, and everything in between - AWS offers specialised services that deliver the best value for money, scalability and low cost.

Scalable data lakes

AWS-based data lakes, backed by the unrivalled availability of Amazon S3, can provide the scalability and flexibility needed for different ways of processing data and analyses to work together. Create and store data lakes in AWS to get more detailed analytical insights than traditional data warehouses provide.

Designed with benefit and performance in mind

AWS analytics services are specifically designed to help you quickly derive useful insights from your data using the most appropriate tools, and offer the best performance, scalability, and cost for your needs.

AWS analytics: modern data application strategy (2:15)

Serverless technology and ease of use

AWS offers the majority of serverless data analytics capabilities in the cloud, including data storage and integration, analytics

big data and real-time data, and much more. The underlying infrastructure is managed by us, allowing you to focus solely on your own application.

Universal access to data, security and management

AWS enables security, control and validation policies to be centrally defined and managed according to industry and location-specific rules. In addition, AWS ensures that data can be accessed and stored securely regardless of location.

Machine learning integration

AWS offers native ML integration within specialised analytics services. You can create, train and deploy machine learning models using familiar SQL commands, without any prior experience in ML.

Hybrid cloud storage

AWS Storage Gateway helps you create hybrid cloud storage by complementing your existing storage environment with the reliability and scalability of Amazon S3. Use this service to extend local storage workloads to the cloud for processing, then load the results back in. Move infrequently used or less valuable data from primary storage to the cloud to reduce costs and expand local resources, preserving the investment you've made. Or simply use it to move data step-by-step to S3 for backups or migration projects.

Cloud application data

Amazon S3 provides high performance and availability, as well as easy scalability and support for fast mobile and web applications. S3 lets you add any amount of content and then access it from any location. So you can deploy applications faster and attract new customers.

Disaster recovery

Amazon S3 global infrastructure is highly reliable and secure. It is equipped with proven disaster recovery solutions that provide the highest data protection. Cross-region replication (CRR) automatically replicates each S3 object to a target bin in another AWS region.

Benefits of the Amazon S3 and Amazon Glacier

The most reliable and resilient platform for your data

Amazon S3 and Amazon Glacier run on the world's largest <u>global cloud</u>

infrastructure, consisting of availability zones and regions around the world. Compared to using a single data centre, these availability zones provide workload applications and databases with increased availability, resiliency and scalability. Data recorded in S3 is stored in three Availability Zones and on multiple devices in each Availability Zone, resulting in 99.999999999% reliability.

High performance on a huge scale

Amazon S3 is the largest object storage service of any cloud infrastructure provider, with total storage capacity that, as noted in a Gartner report, "eclipses other providers" of cloud infrastructure. The S3 service automatically scales performance so that an application does not slow down as data processing speeds increase. Applications can be deployed that reach more users faster because S3 allows any amount of content to be stored and accessed from anywhere.

Data queries without extraction

Amazon S3 is the only cloud storage platform that enables sophisticated big data analytics using directly stored data without having to extract and load it into a separate analytics system. Data queries in S3 can be run without any additional infrastructure using Amazon Athena or Amazon Redshift Spectrum and only pay for the queries executed. This makes the ability to analyse large amounts of unstructured data available to anyone who can use SQL and makes the process more cost-effective than traditional data extraction, transformation and loading (ETL) technologies.

Simple and flexible data transfer

There are a large number of options for transferring data to and from Amazon S3 and Amazon Glacier services. The S3 service's simple and robust APIs make it easy to transfer data over the Internet. Amazon S3 Transfer Acceleration is ideal for large objects that need to be transferred between nodes that are geographically dispersed over significant distances. AWS Direct Connect provides consistent high bandwidth and low latency for transferring large amounts of data to the AWS platform using a dedicated network connection. You can use AWS Snowball and AWS Snowball Edge appliances to transfer petabytes of data, and AWS Snowmobile to transfer even more data. AWS Storage Gateway provides a physical or virtual appliance that can be used locally to easily move entire volumes or individual files to the AWS cloud.

Convenient features for full-featured management

Once you upload your data to Amazon S3 and Amazon Glacier, you are provided with a full set of cloud-based capabilities related to storage management and administration. The S3 service allows you to use policies to ensure compliance with financial goals, regulatory requirements, and corporate policies. The S3 Service's powerful policy engine means you can manage your storage based on business objectives, rather than relying on disparate capabilities offered by different legacy solution providers.

The widest range of security and compliance options

Amazon S3 and Amazon Glacier help protect your data from both internal and external threats and ensure compliance by supporting more security standards and compliance certifications than any other cloud platform. S3 and Glacier services support a variety of certification options including PCI DSS, HIPAA/HITECH, FedRAMP, SEC Rule 17-a-4, EU Data Protection Directive, FISMA, and many others that are suitable for virtually any agency in the world.

Huge and diverse community of partners

In addition to integration with most AWS services, the Amazon S3 Partner Network includes tens of thousands of consultants/system integrators and technology partners/independent software vendors in the AWS Partner Network who have adapted their services and software to work with S3 solutions such as backup and recovery, archiving and disaster recovery. Meanwhile, the AWS Marketplace features more than 3,500 applications in 35 categories from more than 1,100 independent software vendors. More than ten thousand new partners have joined the AWS Partner Network in the past 12 months, including thousands of new technology and consulting partners.

Analysing cloud technologies

Cloud computing technologies are as follows:

Equipment:

▶ hardware virtualisation;

▶ information and computing centres, clusters;

▶ network connections, the Internet.

Software:

▶ distributed file systems;

▶ cloud databases and other storage technologies (e.g. distributed caching systems);

▶ means of load balancing in the network nodes;

▶ tools for processing data in a cloud environment;

▶ webAPIs and web services.

Big data processing and some tasks

Nowadays, graphs are widely used for data modelling in various subject areas to represent mutual relations of objects. The **ever-increasing data volumes of these applications lead to the need to use scalable platforms and parallel computing architectures to efficiently process very large data sets arising from graph analysis**. Cloud computing is used to solve graph-related problems in a number of subject areas: **semantic search, social networks, knowledge bases, photonic crystal modelling, DNA sequence searching, etc.** There are also many problems not directly related to graphs. Let us consider some of the challenges faced by developers of cloud services and by those who use them.

Challenges of resource allocation and utilisation

When organising computational processes in networks with cloud infrastructure, **objects are virtual machines, services, programs, data sets, requests; positions are computational nodes, memory devices, places in execution queues.** In this case, a number of quantitative characteristics are considered: the intensity of incoming requests and the degree of loading of central devices, the intensity of inter-machine interaction through network adapters, etc. Indicator-type characteristics may also be taken into account, for example, the availability of a necessary packet on a given computational node. Then there arise, generally speaking, optimisation problems on graphs related to resource allocation and utilisation and scheduling. For example, we need to solve a given application problem and at the same time minimise the sum of traffic between all pairs of cloud nodes. **To solve these problems, various, usually approximate, methods are used: optimisation, game**

theory-based, statistical, and machine learning methods.
MapReduce model of computation
MapReduce is a distributed computing model proposed by Google, used for parallel computing over very large amounts of data, several petabytes, datasets in computer clusters... More precisely, **MapReduce is a framework for organising computational processes on distributed systems containing a large number of computers called nodes.**

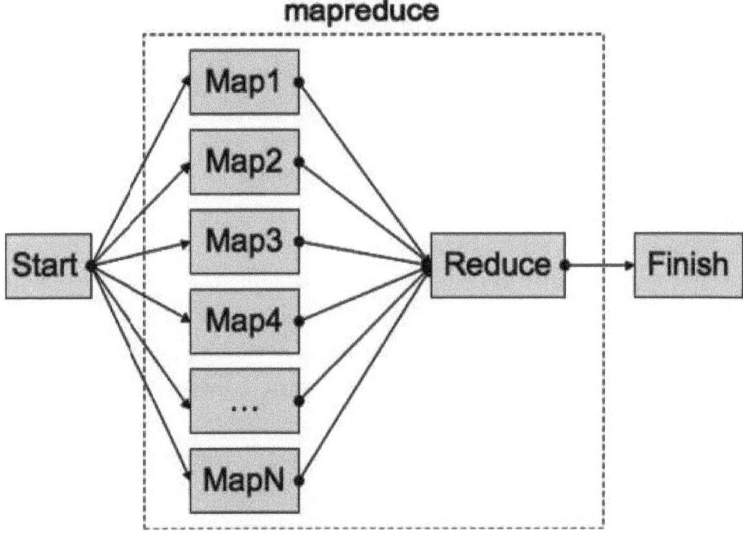

Fig.8.1 MapReduce functioning scheme

MapReduce can rightfully be called the main technology of Big Data, as it is initially oriented on parallel computing in distributed clusters. The essence of MapReduce consists in dividing an information array into parts, parallel processing of each part on a separate node and final integration of all results.
Programmes that   use MapReduce automatically
are parallelised and executed on distributed cluster nodes, with the runtime system itself taking care of implementation details (splitting input data into parts, dividing tasks by cluster nodes, handling failures and communicating between distributed computers). Thanks to this, programmers can easily and efficiently use the resources of distributed Big Data systems.

The authors of this computational model are Google employees Jeffrey Dean (Jeffrey Dean) and Sanjay Ghemawat (Sanjay Ghemawat), who took as a basis two procedures of functional programming: **map**, which applies the desired function to each element of the list, and **reduce,** combining the results of **map**. During the computation process, the set of input key/value pairs is converted into the set of output key/value pairs.

The name MapReduce was originally patented by Google Corporation, but as Big Data technologies have evolved, it has become a common term in the world of Big Data. Today, there are many different commercial and free products that use this distributed computing model: Apache Hadoop, Apache CouchDB, MongoDB, MySpace Qizmt and other Big Data frameworks and libraries written in different programming languages. Some of the other best known MapReduce implementations include the following:

• Greenplum is a commercial implementation with support for Python, Perl, SQL and other languages;

• GridGain is a free and open source implementation in Java;

• Phoenix is a C implementation using shared memory;

• MapReduce is implemented in NVIDIA GPUs using CUDA;

• Qt Concurrent is a simplified version of the framework, implemented in C++, for distributing a task across multiple cores on the same computer;

• CouchDB uses MapReduce to define views on top of distributed documents;

• Skynet is an open source implementation in the Ruby language;

• Disco is an implementation from Nokia whose core is written in Erlang and applications can be developed in Python;

• The Hive framework is an open source add-on from Facebook that allows you to combine a MapReduce approach with SQL-like data access;

• Qizmt is an open source implementation from MySpace written in C#;

• DryadLINQ is an implementation from Microsoft Research based on PLINQ and Dryad.

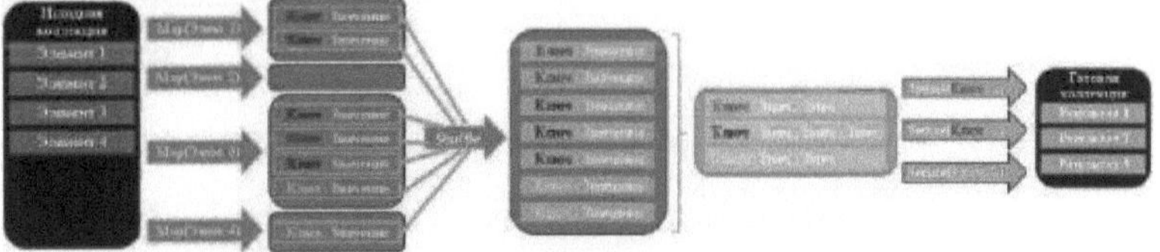

Fig.8.2 MapReduce functioning

MapReduce is the separation, parallel processing and convolution of distributed results

The MapReduce operation consists of two steps: Map and Reduce.

• In the Map step, the input data is pre-processed. To do this, one of the computers, called the **master node,** receives the task input data, divides it into parts, and passes it to other computers, called **worker nodes,** for pre-processing.

• **At the Reduce-step the pre-processed data is "merged".** The main node receives answers from the worker nodes and forms the result, i.e. the solution of the problem, on their basis. **Within the framework of this paradigm, Dijkstra's algorithm for finding the shortest path in a graph, various algorithms for finding significant vertices in a graph, nearest neighbour method, Bayesian classification algorithm, etc. have been implemented.**

To process the data according to the MapReduce computational model, you must define both of these functions, specify the input and output file names, and the processing parameters.

The computational model itself consists of a 3-step combination of the above functions:

1. **Map** - preprocessing of input data in the form of a large list of values. The cluster master node receives this list, divides it into parts and passes it to the worker nodes. Each worker node then applies the Map function to the local data and writes the result in key-value format to temporary storage.

2. **Shuffle**, where worker nodes redistribute data based on the keys previously created by the Map function, so that all data of one key lies on one worker node.

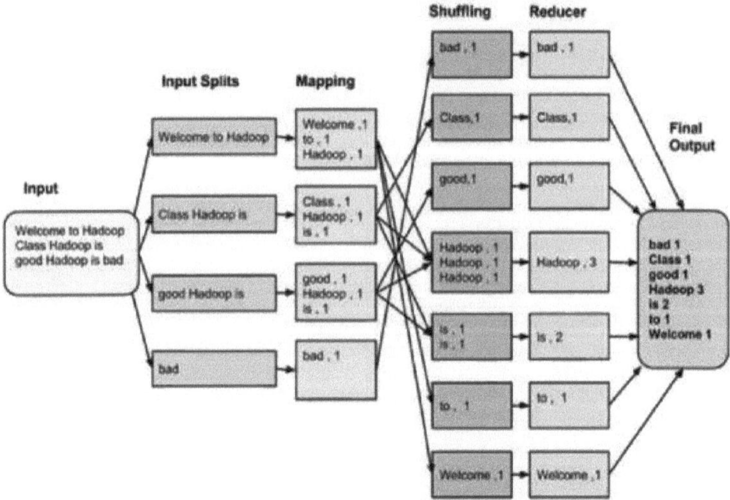

Fig.8.3 MapReduce working principle

3. **Reduce** - parallel processing by each worker node of each group of data by key order and "gluing" the results to the master node. The master node receives intermediate answers from worker nodes and passes them to free nodes to perform the next step. The result obtained after all the necessary steps is the solution to the original problem.

Stages of calculation:

1. preparation of data for the Map() procedure on the system nodes, elimination of duplicate data;
2. execution of the Map() code defined by the user;
3. data reorganisation (*shuffle*) to perform the Reduce() function;
4. execution of the Reduce() code defined by the user;
5. output of the result obtained.

MapReduce Characteristics

Features:

► The Reduce procedure can be executed in multiple steps as data arrives at each node and when aggregating data across different nodes.

► The MapReduce method is effective for processing large amounts of data (~Gb-TB).

Applications:

► distributed search and indexing;

► distributed sorting;

► obtaining statistics on documents in distributed storages;

► mathematical applications (e.g. singular value decomposition of matrices); machine learning (e.g. document clustering, machine learning)

Example of an algorithm

The canonical example of an application written with *MapReduce* is a pseudocode program that counts the number of different words in a set of documents:

```
// A function used by worker nodes in the Map step to process key-value
// pairs from the input stream
void map(String name, String document):
// Input data:
// name - name of the document
// document - content of the document
for each word w in document:
EmitIntermediate(w, "1");
// The function used by worker nodes in the Reduce-step to process key-value
// pairs obtained in the Map-step
void reduce(String word, Iterator partialCounts):
// Input data:
// word - word
// partialCounts - list of grouped intermediate results. The  number of
// records in partialCounts  is the required value
int result = 0;
```

```
for each v in partialCounts: result += parseInt(v);
Emit(AsString(result));
```
This code breaks each document into words at the Map step, and returns pairs where the key is the word itself and the value is "1". If the same word occurs multiple times in a document, the preprocessing of that document will result in as many of these pairs as the number of times the word occurs.

Example 2.

INPUT: string "foo bar baz bar"

NEED TO EXIT: { foo: 1, bar: 2, baz: 1 } *MapReduce*

1. Line breakdown:

['foo', 1] ['bar', 1] ['baz', 1] ['bar', 1]

2. Sorting:

bar, 1

bar, 1

baz, 1

foo, 1

3. Combining:

bar, (1,1) baz, (1) foo, (1)

4. Folding:

bar, 2

baz, 1

foo, 1

Python:
```
words = ["foo", "bar", "baz"]
def map1(word):
return [word, 1]
arr = ["foo", [1,1]]
def reduce1(arr):
return [ arr[0], sum(arr[1]) ] ]
```
MapReduce

Sorting by frequency:

1. In ascending order=> multiply by -1

[word, 15] -> map() returns -> [-15, word]

[word2, 15] -> map() returns -> [-15, word2]

[word3, 120] -> map() returns -> [-120, word3]

[word4, 1] -> map() returns -> [-1, word4]

2. Grouping

-120, (word3) -15, (word, word2) <-- two words on a line - grouped everything by the first key! -1, (word4)

3. Multiplication by -1 and division

120, word3 15, word, 15, word2 1, word4

The library combines all pairs with the same key and passes them to the input of the *reduce* function, which has to add them up to get the total number of occurrences of a given word in all documents. Calls to the Map operation are distributed across multiple machines by automatically dividing the input data into a set of M parts. The input parts can be processed in parallel by multiple machines. Calls to the Reduce operation are distributed by partitioning the intermediate key space into R parts using a partitioning function (e.g., hash(key)modR). The number of R parts and the partition function are specified by the user. The following diagram (Fig. 8.4) shows the complete process of a *MapReduce* operation in Google's implementation.

When the user programme calls the *MapReduce* function, *the* following sequence of operations takes place (their numbers in the diagram correspond to the list below):

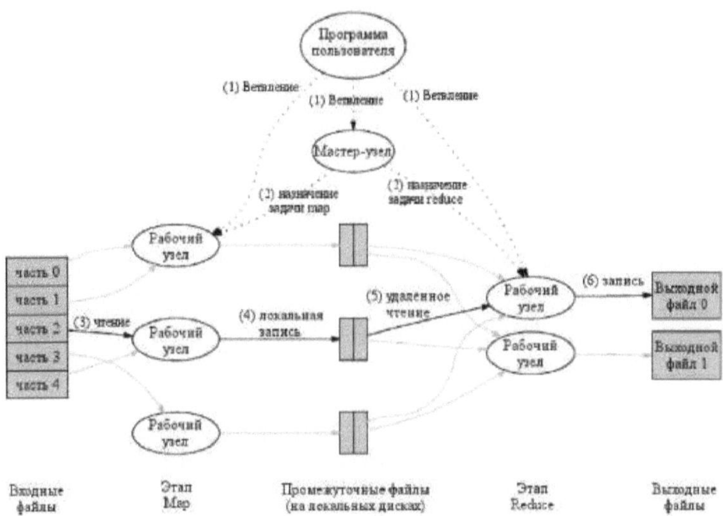

Fig.8.4: A detailed overview of how Google's implementation works

When the user programme calls the *MapReduce* function, *the* following sequence of operations takes place (their numbers in the diagram correspond to the list below):

1. First, the *MapReduce* library in the user's programme divides the input files into M parts, each of which typically occupies between 16 and 64 megabytes (this parameter can be set by the user). It then runs multiple copies of the programme on the cluster.

2.   One of the copies of the programme (master) is special, it assigns work to the other instances (workers). In total, M map tasks and R reduce tasks need to be assigned. The master searches for inactive worker instances and assigns one task to each of them.

3.   The working instance of the programme to which the map task has been assigned reads the contents of the relevant part of the input data, parses it, and passes each element to the user's Map function. Intermediate key-value pairs are then stored in memory.

4.   At intervals, the saved pairs are written to the local disc and split into R regions by the split function. The locations of these pairs on the disc are passed back to the master, which is responsible for further communicating these locations to the worker instances.

5.   When a worker instance is notified of the location of intermediate data, it reads the data from the local drives of the instances that applied the map function. When all the data is read, it is sorted by key and grouped together. If the amount of data is too large, external sorting is used.

6.   The worker instance walks through the sorted intermediate data and passes each unique key and its corresponding list of values to the Reduce function. The result is appended to the final file for that piece of intermediate data.

7.   When all map and reduce tasks have been completed, the *MapReduce* call will be terminated and a return back to the user code will occur.

After successful completion of processing, the output will be available in R result files (one file per reduce task) with user-defined names. Typically, users do not need to merge these R files into one - it is often the case that these files are passed to another *MapReduce* call already as input, or are processed in other distributed applications that are also passed multiple files as input.

Advantages and disadvantages of MapReduce

MapReduce can be called the foundation of Big Data, because this technology allows processing huge amounts of information in parallel in distributed clusters. This computing model is supported by many different commercial and free products: Apache <u>Hadoop, Spark, Greenplum, Hive, MongoDB,</u> Phoenix,

DryadLINQ and other Big Data frameworks and libraries written in different programming languages. Today we will look at the main advantages and disadvantages of this technology and talk about how leading Big Data developers try to get around its main problems.

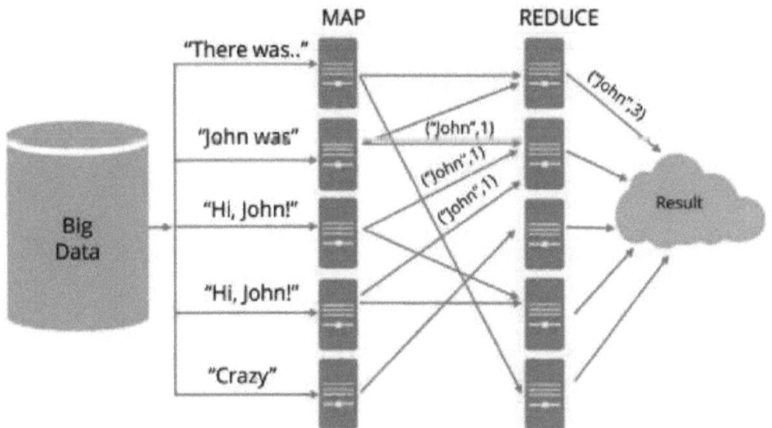

Fig.8.5 Big Data and MapReduce

Main advantages of the model

The key advantages of MapReduce are as follows:

• **the possibility of distributed execution of** preprocessing (map) and reducing (reduce) **operations of a** large amount of data. In this case map functions work independently of each other and can be executed in parallel on different nodes of the cluster. Note that in practice the number of simultaneously executed map functions is limited by the source of input data and the number of processors used. Similarly, multiple nodes perform reduce after each of them has processed all map function results with one specific key value.

• **Fast processing of large amounts of data** due to the distribution of operations according to the principle described above. For example, MapReduce can sort an entire petabyte of data in just a couple of hours.

• **fault tolerance and rapid recovery from failures**: when a worker node that performs a map or reduce operation fails, its work is automatically transferred to another worker node if the input data for the operation is available.

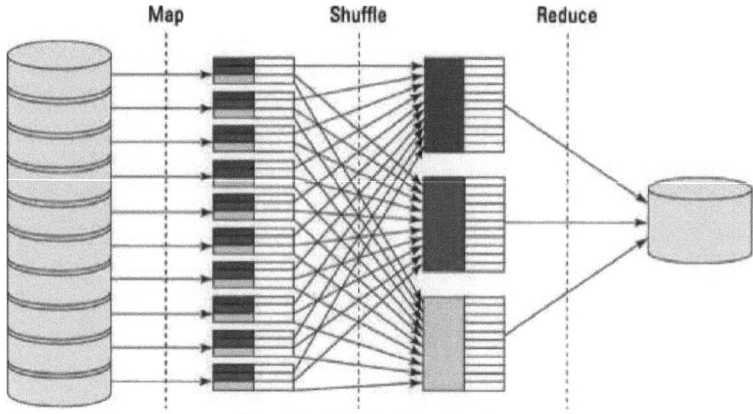

Fig.8.5 Classic MapReduce

Disadvantages and alternatives to BIG DATA solutions

First of all, we note that the first version of the MapReduce framework implemented in Apache Hadoop v1.0 was characterised by the following limitations:

• Apache Hadoop **cluster scalability limit**: no more than 4K compute nodes and about 40K parallel jobs;

• **strong interconnectivity of the** distributed computing framework and client libraries implementing the distributed algorithm;

• **Single points of failure** and inability to be used in environments with high reliability requirements;

• **version compatibility issues**:the need

One-time update of all compute nodes in the cluster when the Hadoop platform is upgraded (new version or service pack is installed).

These limitations have been addressed in the new MapReduce 2.0 version released in 2012 through changes to the ResourceManager and the application coordinator scheduler

ApplicationMaster, as well as the emergence of YARN (Yet Another Resource Negotiator). This distributed application execution framework provides components and APIs for developing distributed applications of various types, providing resource allocation in response to requests from running applications and responsibility for tracking their execution status.

In particular, the ResourceManager is responsible for cluster resource management, and the ApplicationMaster is responsible for application lifecycle planning/coordination. In this case, each compute node is divided into an arbitrary number of *Container* containers containing a predefined number of resources: CPU, RAM, etc., which are monitored by the

NodeManager.

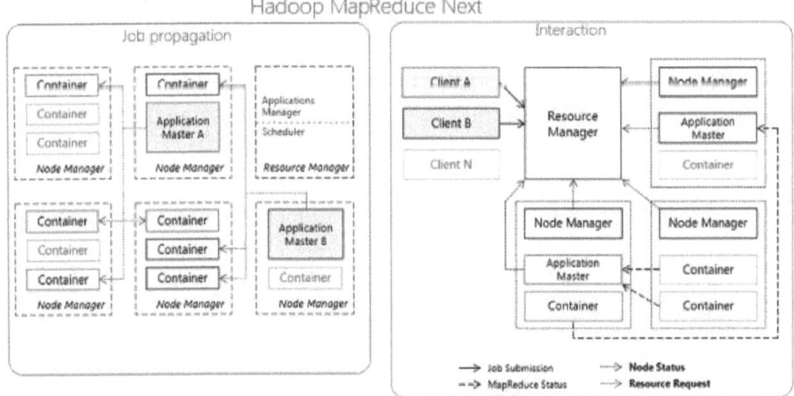

Fig.8.6. MapReduce 2.0 working principle

Nevertheless, these innovations **have** not eliminated the **shortcomings of MapReduce due to the architectural features of this computational model**:

• **insufficiently high performance** - classical technology, in particular, implemented in the Apache Hadoop kernel, processes data acyclically in batch mode. In this case, Reduce functions will not start until all Map processes are completed. All operations are performed on a read-write cycle from the hard disc, which causes latency in information processing.

• **limited application** - continuing the above-mentioned disadvantage, high latency of distributed computing, acceptable in batch processing mode, does not allow using classic MapReduce for real-time streaming processing, repetitive queries and iterative algorithms on the same dataset, as in Machine Learning tasks. Other Big Data frameworks, notably Apache Spark and Flink, have been created to address this problem inherent in Apache Hadoop.

For example, unlike the classic Apache Hadoop kernel processor with a two-level MapReduce concept based on disk storage, Spark uses specialised primitives for recurrent processing in RAM. This makes many tasks computationally faster. For example, multiple access to user data loaded into memory allows efficient work with Machine Learning algorithms.

Thus, the **advantages and disadvantages of MapReduce determine the specifics of the applied use of this computational model**. In particular, this technology is not used in its pure form in streaming Big Data systems, where it is required to quickly process large amounts of continuously arriving information in real time. In practice, this is the case in platforms Internet of Things. However, if the requirement for fast data processing is not critical and the business application is suitable for batch data processing, such as in ETL systems or web page indexing, MapReduce can handle these tasks perfectly.

Apache Hadoop

Hadoop is a free Java framework that supports the execution of distributed applications running on large clusters built on conventional hardware.

Supports the MapReduce paradigm.

Apache Hadoop shell for distributed data storage and processing written in Java.

The application is divided into a large number of small jobs, each of which can be executed on any of the nodes in the cluster.

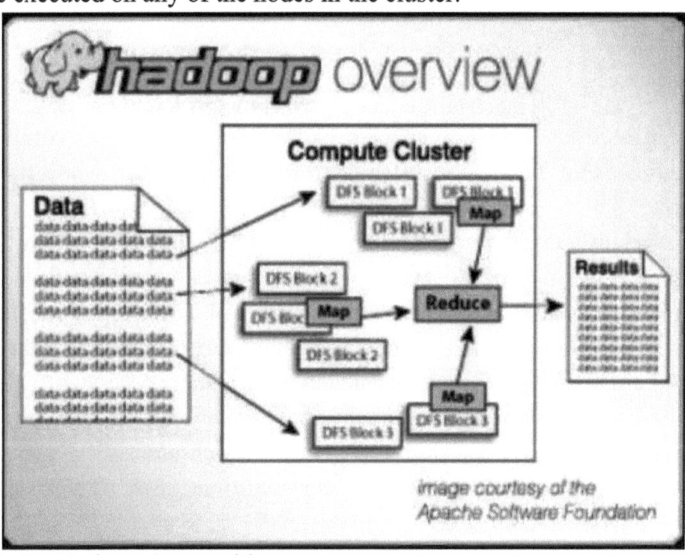

Figure 8.7 Hadoop Composition

Modules:

▶ HDFS is a distributed file system for data storage;

▶ MapReduce JobTracker (central job management module), TaskTracker (execution of Map and Reduce procedures);

▶ job scheduler.

Hadoop plug-ins

▶ **File systems** (available through plugins).

▶ **NoSQL database** HBase (installed on top of HDFS).

▶ Apache Spark architecture for performing **distributed data processing**, an alternative to MapReduce.

▶ Apache Mahout is a **machine learning** library written in Java.

▶ Apache Pig is a high-level **platform for creating MapReduce-type jobs** based on Pig Latin (SQL) procedural language and custom functions in Python, Java, JavaScript.

▶ Apache Hive **infrastructure for data processing** using the HiveQL query language, which is translated into a set of jobs for Hadoop.

▶ Apache ZooKeeper **centralised coordination server** in distributed systems.

Data processing

Machine learning extracting useful information from data using optimisation/mat statistics techniques:

▶ regression (polynomial, MARS);

▶ classification (Bayesian methods, decision trees, SVM, bousting, ...);

▶ structural recognition (image processing, text processing, ...);

▶ clustering (k-means, Gaussian mixtures);

▶ dimensionality reduction (singular value decomposition and other methods).

Reverse data indexing preparation of an index for full-text search in a large volume of documents.

Analysing data with *Hadoop*

The Windows Azure HDInsight (Hadoop) service is a cloud service that offers an ecosystem and on-demand *Hadoop* cluster creation. Using the *Windows Azure* portal, *Hadoop* clusters up to 32 nodes in size can be created and deployed (it should be clarified that at the time of writing, the *Windows AzureHDInsight service* is in a closed *Preview* version). In addition to creating *MapReduce* tasks, the developer has access to an interactive console that allows writing data queries in *JavaScript* and *Hive*.

MapReduce is a parallel and distributed solution developed by *Google* Corporation for processing large data sets and is actively used in areas such as, for example, search engines. *MapReduce*, or *M/R*, consists of two component functions, *Map* and *Reduce*. The first function, *Map*, is used to compute key-value sets. *Reduce* is a function that takes the results of a *Map* function computation and applies another function to them. The *M/R* approach assumes that there are no direct dependencies between the data, which simplifies the parallelisation process. The master node distributes *M/R* tasks to *Map* and *Reduce* handlers, collecting information. All key-value pairs with identical key value are sent to a single handler for processing.

A typical use case for *MapReduce*, and hence *Hadoop*, is analysing log files. It is common for log files to grow to very large sizes, with all files adhering to a strict data syntax that allows processing logic to be applied to these files.

Despite the simplicity of processing, if log files contain a very large number of records, it can take a long time to process them on a single computer.

MapReduce can be used to split large log files into parts. The *Map* function searches for unique occurrences of records (e.g. *web* pages). Each time a *web page is* in the file, the *Reduce* function receives a key-value, where the key is the *web page* and the value is 1. The *Reduce* function handlers aggregate the counts for each of the *web* pages, and as a result, the user gets the total number of entries for each of the *web pages*.

The service is based on *HDFS* (*Hadoop Distributed File System*), implemented on a cluster of *Hadoop* nodes of two types - *Data Node* and *Name Node*. Such a cluster can be both homogeneous (with unified characteristics of nodes) and heterogeneous (a large number of nodes of different characteristics). *Name Nodes* contain information about which *Data Node contains a* particular replica (replicas are used to ensure high reliability and redundancy), and present this information to the client. When a fragment replica fails, one of its secondary replicas is assigned as the primary replica. Scalability is achieved by parallel processing of tasks. *Task Trackers* are nodes that store input task fragments (files) and launch *MapRedurce* execution instances, while a node called *Job Tracker* coordinates these execution instances. In various real-world tasks, the *Hadoop/HDInsight* ecosystem consists of many more components and integration modules with other software and data formats.

Figure 8.8: *Hadoop/HDInsight* ecosystem

The data used by *HDInsight* in tasks is stored in *WindowsAzure Storage* in blobs and is retrieved for processing using the *MapReduce* paradigm by the master node, which then distributes the tasks according to the specified logic to the handlers. For this reason, for the cluster to work, you must create and configure a *Windows Azure* storage account and create the cluster as close to the geographical location of the storage as possible (to avoid increased latency).

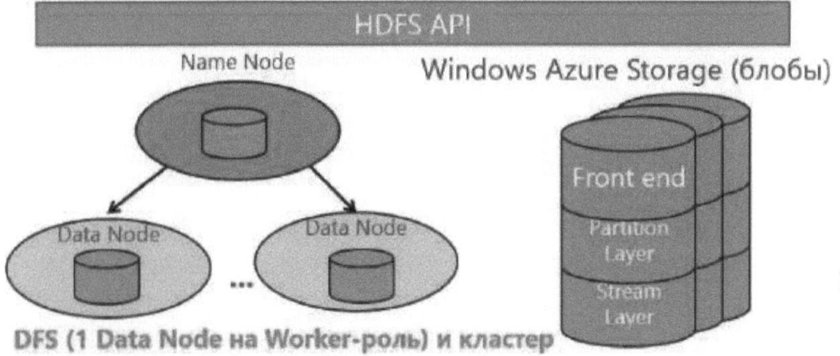

Fig.8.9. Access to the *HDInsight* repository

***HDInsight* ecosystem**

As outlined above, the *HDInsight* service provides a cloud-based big data management service. *HDInsight* has its own implementations of *Hive* and *Pig*, which are used for data processing and storage, respectively, and is also able to integrate with existing powerful *BI* tools developed by *Microsoft*: *SQL Server Analysis Services, Reporting Services, PowerPivot, Excel*.

Talking about what *Pig is*, it should be clarified that *Pig is* a high-level platform that provides big data processing capabilities in *Hadoop* clusters. *Pig* consists of a special *Pig Latin* query language that executes to data sets in the console and is capable of integrating *User DefinedFunctions* (*UDFs*) in *Java, Python, C#* and *JavaScript*.

Hive is a distributed storage service "on top" of *HDFS* and provides an interface to interact with data using *SQL* queries in *HiveQL* (a sub-dialect of *SQL*) and a relational model. Similar to *Pig*, *Hive* transforms a query in its own language into *MapReduce* tasks.

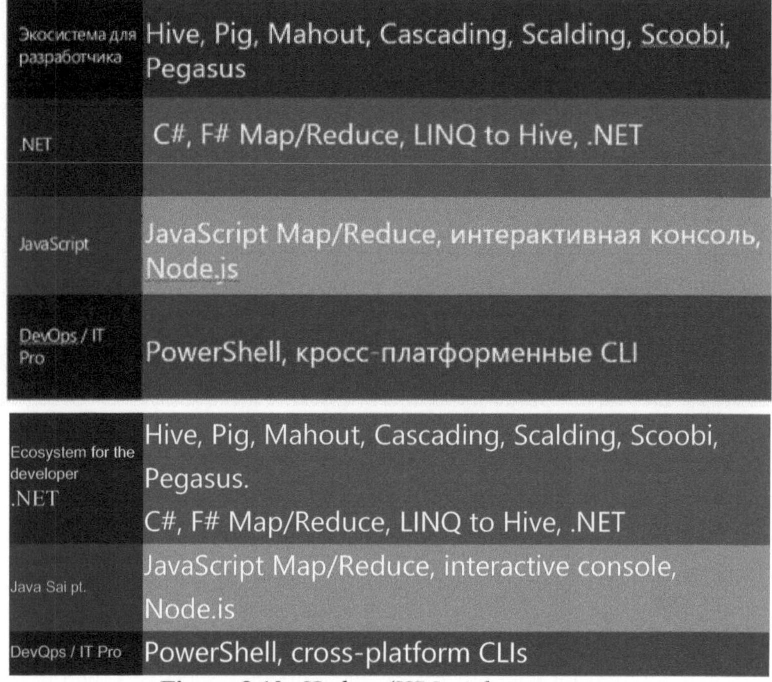

Figure 8.10: *Hadoop/HDInsight* ecosystem

HDInsight's functionality also ensures that the developer can use familiar tools such as *Powershell*, *.NET*, *Java*, *F#*, *Javascript* and *Node.js* to develop, manage and monitor what is happening on the cluster. *HDInsight* can also be installed in its local version on a *Microsoft Windows Server* product.

Distributed databases

The foundation for cloud infrastructure is data storage. For this purpose, both unstructured storage (i.e., distributed file systems) and databases with different degrees of structuring are used. The main obstacle in the construction of distributed storage is formulated in the form of the so-called **CAP-Brewer** theorem.

The CAP theorem (also known as **Brewer's theorem**) is a heuristic statement that it is possible for any distributed computing implementation to provide at most two of the following three properties:

▶ data *consistency* (**c** *onsistency*) - in all computational nodes at one moment of time the data do not contradict each other;

▶ *vailability* - any request to a distributed system ends with **a** correct response, but with no guarantee that the responses of all nodes in the system coincide;

▶ **p** *artition tolerance* - splitting of a distributed system into several isolated sections does not lead to incorrect response from each of the sections.

The acronym *CAP* in the name of the theorem is formed from the first letters of the English names of these three properties.

Since distributed systems used in the cloud must be scalable, AP storage (with possible data inconsistency at some time intervals) and CP storage (with "lost" queries) are distinguished. Ordinary relational databases, corresponding to the AC signature, are not well suited for cloud storage (although there are adapted modifications, such as MySQL Cluster).

The databases used in cloud computing can be categorised by the data schemas used. Most of the raw data for the cloud is either not structured at all (e.g., images) or poorly structured (e.g., documents in JSON format). Thus, storing information in relational tables is inefficient; instead of tables, a NoSQL (not only SQL) approach is used, which focuses on the lack of rigid data schema and normalisation. There are four main types of NoSQL databases according to the type of stored objects:

▶ key-value pairs (often used for distributed data caching);

▶ data columns;

▶ semi-structured documents like JSON;

▶ graphs of relationships between entities.

Cloud systems use specific computation methods to process data. One of the most common models of such computing is MapReduce, proposed by Google.

Disadvantages of relational databases for cloud applications:

▶ impossibility of linear horizontal *scaling* (*scaling out* linear performance growth with increasing number of nodes), poor compatibility with distributed systems;

▶ absence or insufficiency of inbuilt caching mechanisms;

▶ fragmentation when storing large amounts of data;

▶ rigidity of the data schema, the need to structure incoming information;

▶ transactions to maintain data consistency, slowing down the system;

▶ performance-reducing operations of data normalisation and table joins (SQL JOIN operator). NoSQL

Definition

NoSQL (not only SQL) data model for distributed data storage, which is different from the relational algebra of traditional DBMSs.

Characteristics:

▶ absence of a rigid data schema, designing data structures according to predefined query templates (not vice versa, as in RDBMS);

► simplification of data structure compared to relational tables, lack of normalisation;

► refusal of transactions in favour of *delayed consistency;*

► built-in support for distributed architecture and (often) caching.

Data structures in NoSQL

Types of databases (from simple to complex):

► **Key-value pairs.** Used for caching; often data is stored exclusively in RAM.

Examples: Redis; memcached.

► *Column-oriented.* They are used to store simply structured data when quick access is required.

Examples: Apache Cassandra, Apache HBase.

► **Graph-based.** Store relationships between entities (e.g. followers / followed by on Twitter).

Examples: Neo4j; OrientDB.

► **Document-oriented.** They are used to store arbitrary documents with a schema defined by a serialisation format (e.g. JSON).

Examples: Apache CouchDB, MongoDB.

Virtualisation and cloud computing

Virtualisation and cloud computing are related technologies. They are needed to create efficient working environments from abstract resources. Thus, virtualisation is the creation of a number of individual resources or simulated spaces based on a single physical machine. Cloud computing represents workloads that reside in the cloud, which refers to an IT environment capable of abstracting, aggregating, and simultaneously applying scalable resources on the Internet. That is, looking ahead we can say that virtualisation is the foundation of cloud computing.

The core technology for cloud computing is virtualisation. Virtualisation is the division of one physical server into multiple logical servers. Once the physical server is split, each logical server behaves like a physical server and can run the operating system and applications independently. Many popular companies such as VmWare and Microsoft provide virtualisation services, where instead of using your personal computer for storage and computing, you use their virtual server. These are fast, cost effective and less labour intensive.

For software developers and testers, virtualisation is very useful because it allows the developer to write code that runs in many different environments and, more importantly, to test that code.

Virtualisation is mainly used for three main purposes: **1) network virtualisation 2) server virtualisation 3) storage virtualisation**

Network virtualisation: is a method of pooling available resources on a network by dividing the available bandwidth into channels, each channel independent of the others, and each channel is independent of the others and can be assigned to a specific server or device in real time.

Storage virtualisation: is the consolidation of physical storage from multiple networked storage devices into what appears to be a single storage device managed from a central console. Storage virtualisation is commonly used in storage area networks (SANs).

Server virtualisation is the masking of server resources such as processors, RAM, operating system, etc. from the server users. The goal of server virtualisation is to increase resource sharing and reduce the load and complexity of computing on the part of users.

Virtualisation is the key to unlocking a cloud system, which is why virtualisation is so important to the cloud, it separates software from hardware. For example, PCs can use virtual memory to borrow additional memory from the hard drive. Typically, the hard drive has much more space than memory. Although virtual discs are slower than real memory, if managed properly, the substitution works fine. Similarly, there is software that can simulate an entire computer, which means that 1 computer can perform functions equal to 20 computers.

Virtualisation technologies

According to statistics, the average level of processor capacity utilisation in Windows servers does not exceed 10%, in Unix-systems this indicator is better, but nevertheless on average it does not exceed 10%.

exceeds 20 per cent. The low efficiency of server utilisation is explained by the "one application - one server" approach widely used since the early 90s, i.e. each time a company acquires a new server to deploy a new application. Obviously, in practice, this means a rapid increase in the server fleet and, as a consequence, higher costs for its administration, power consumption and cooling, as well as the need for additional premises for the installation of more and more servers and the purchase of licences for the server OS.

Virtualisation of physical server resources allows flexible distribution between applications, each of which "sees" only the resources assigned to it and "considers" that it has a separate server, i.e. in this case the "one server - several applications" approach is implemented, but without reducing the performance, availability and security of server applications. In addition, virtualisation solutions make it possible to run different operating systems in partitions by emulating their system calls to server hardware resources.

Figure 9.1. Virtualisation involves running multiple virtual computers on one physical computer

At the heart of virtualisation is the ability of a single computer to do the work of multiple computers by spreading its resources across multiple environments. With virtual servers and virtual desktops, you can host multiple operating systems and multiple applications in a single location. In this way, physical and geographical limitations cease to matter. In addition to saving energy and reducing costs through more efficient use of hardware

104

resources, virtualised infrastructure provides high levels of resource availability, more efficient management, enhanced security and improved disaster recovery.

In a broad sense, virtualisation is the concealment of the actual implementation of a process or object from its true representation to the user. The product of virtualisation is something usable that actually has a more complex or quite different structure from that perceived when working with the object. In other words, there is a separation of the representation from the realisation of something. Virtualisation is designed to abstract the software from the hardware.

In computing, the term "virtualisation" usually refers to abstracting computing resources and providing the user with a system that "encapsulates" (hides within itself) its own implementation.

Simply put, the user is working with a convenient representation of the object, and it does not matter to him how the object is actually arranged.

Right now, the ability to run multiple virtual machines on a single physical machine is generating a lot of interest among computer professionals, not only because it increases the flexibility of IT infrastructure, but also because virtualisation actually saves money.

The history of virtualisation technology development goes back more than forty years. IBM was the first to think about creating virtual environments for various user tasks, then still in mainframes. In the 1960s, virtualisation was of purely scientific interest and was an original solution to isolate computer systems within a single physical computer. After the advent of personal computers, interest in virtualisation waned somewhat due to the rapid development of operating systems, which placed adequate demands on the hardware of the time. However, the rapid growth of computer hardware capacities at the end of the nineties of the last century made the IT community think about software platform virtualisation technologies again.

In 1999, VMware introduced x86-based system virtualisation technology as an effective means of transforming x86-based systems into a single, shared and purpose-built hardware infrastructure that provides complete isolation, mobility and a wide choice of operating systems for application environments. VMware was one of the first companies to make a serious bet on virtualisation alone. As time has shown, it has proved to be absolutely justified.   Today, WMware offers a comprehensive

VMware vSphere 4, a fourth-generation virtualisation platform that includes both single PC and data centre facilities. A key component of this software suite is the VMware ESX Server hypervisor.

Later, such companies as Parallels (formerly SWsoft), Oracle (Sun Microsystems), Citrix Systems (XenSourse) joined the "battle" for a place in this trendy direction of information technology development.

Microsoft entered the virtualisation market in 2003 with the acquisition of Connectix, launching its first Virtual PC product for desktop PCs. Since then, it has steadily increased the range of offerings in this area and today has almost completed the formation of a virtualisation platform, which includes such solutions as Windows2008 Server R2 with Hyper-V component, Microsoft Application Virtualisation (App-v), Microsoft Virtual Desktop Infrastructure (VDI), Remote Desktop Services, System Center Virtual Machine Manager.

Today, virtualisation vendors offer reliable and easily managed platforms, and the virtualisation market is booming. According to leading experts, virtualisation is now one of the top three most promising computer technologies. Many experts predict that by 2015, about half of all computer systems will be virtualised.

The increased interest in virtualisation technologies at present is not accidental. The computing power of today's processors is growing rapidly, and the question is not even what to spend this power on, but the fact that the current "fashion" for dual-core and multi-core systems, which has already penetrated into personal computers (laptops and desktops), is the best way to realise the rich potential of the ideas of virtualisation of operating systems and applications, bringing the convenience of using a computer to a new qualitative level. Virtualisation technologies are becoming one of the key components (including marketing) in the newest and future Intel and AMD processors, in operating systems from Microsoft and a number of other companies.

Benefits of virtualisation

Here are the main advantages of virtualisation technologies:

1 .Efficient use of computing resources. Instead of 3, or even 10 servers, loaded by 5-20%, you can use one server, used by 50-70%. Among other things, this also saves energy and significantly reduces financial investments: you get one high-tech server that performs the functions of 5-10 servers. With virtualisation, you can achieve much more efficient use of resources, as it pools standard infrastructure resources into a single pool and overcomes the limitations of the outdated one-application-per-server model.

2 .Reduced infrastructure costs: Virtualisation reduces the number of servers and associated IT equipment in a data centre. As a result, maintenance, power and cooling requirements for physical resources are

reduced and much less money is spent on IT.

3   .Reduced software costs. Some software vendors have introduced separate licensing schemes specifically for virtual environments. For example, buying one licence for Microsoft Windows Server 2008 Enterprise, you get the right to use it simultaneously on 1 physical server and 4 virtual servers (within one server), and Windows Server 2008 Datacenter is licensed only for the number of processors and can be used simultaneously on an unlimited number of virtual servers.

4   .Increased system flexibility and responsiveness: Virtualisation offers a new way to manage IT infrastructure and helps IT administrators spend less time on repetitive tasks - such as initiation, configuration, tracking and maintenance. Many system administrators have experienced the unpleasantness when a server "crashes." And you can't, by removing the hard drive, moving it to another server, start everything up as before.... And the installation? Finding drivers, setting up, running... and it all takes time and resources. If you use a virtual server, you can instantly run it on any hardware, and if you don't have such a server, you can download a ready-made virtual machine with the server installed and configured from the libraries supported by hypervisor (virtualisation software) developers.

5   Incompatible applications can run on the same computer. When using virtualisation on the same server, it is possible to install linux and windows servers, gateways, databases and other completely incompatible applications within the same non-virtualised system.

6   .Increase application availability and ensure business continuity: With reliable backup and migration of entire virtual environments without service interruption, you can reduce planned downtime and ensure rapid system recovery in critical situations. "Downing" one virtual server does not result in the loss of the remaining virtual servers. In addition, in case of failure of one physical server, it is possible to automatically replace it with a backup server. And it is not noticeable for users without restarting. This ensures business continuity.

7   .Easy archiving capabilities. Since the hard drive of a virtual machine is usually represented as a file of a specific format located on some physical media, virtualisation provides the ability to easily copy this file to backup media as a means of archiving and backing up the entire virtual machine. The ability to bring up a server completely from the archive is another great feature. And you can bring up a server from the archive without destroying the current server and see the state of affairs for the past period.

8.Increased manageability of the infrastructure: the use of centralised virtual infrastructure management reduces server administration time, provides load balancing and live migration of virtual machines.

Virtual machine

We will call a virtual machine a software or hardware environment that hides the real implementation of some process or object from its visible representation.

A virtual machine is a completely isolated software container that runs its own operating system and applications, just like a physical computer. A virtual machine acts just like a physical computer and contains its own virtual (i.e., software) RAM, hard drive, and network adapter.

The OS cannot distinguish between a virtual machine and a physical machine. The same is true for applications and other computers on the network. Even the virtual machine itself considers itself a "real" computer. Even so, virtual machines consist solely of software components and do not include hardware. This gives them a number of unique advantages over physical hardware.

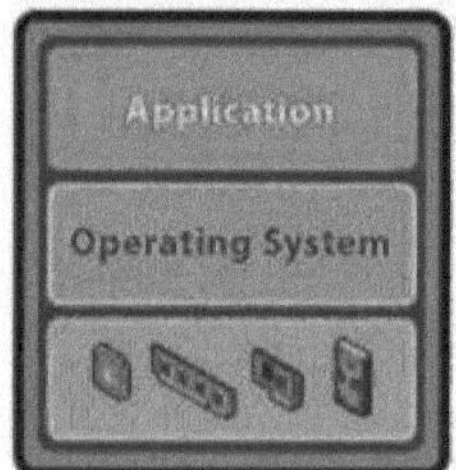

Figure 9.2. Virtual machine

Let's look at the main features of virtual machines in more detail:

1 .Compatibility. Virtual machines are generally compatible with all standard computers. Like a physical computer, a virtual machine runs its own guest operating system and runs its own applications. It also contains all the components that are standard for a physical computer (motherboard, video card, network controller, etc.). Therefore, virtual machines are fully compatible with all standard operating systems, applications and device drivers. A virtual machine can be used to run any software suitable for the corresponding physical computer.

2 .Isolation. Virtual machines are completely isolated from each other as if they were physical computers. Virtual machines can share the physical resources of a single computer and still remain completely isolated from each other as if they were separate physical machines. For example, if there are four virtual machines running on a single physical server and one of them

fails, the availability of the remaining three machines is not affected. Isolation is an important reason for the much higher availability and security of applications running in a virtualised environment compared to applications running on a standard, non-virtualised system.

3   .Encapsulation. Virtual machines completely encapsulate the computing environment. A virtual machine is a software container that binds, or "encapsulates" a complete set of virtual hardware resources, as well as the OS and all of its applications in a software package. Encapsulation makes virtual machines incredibly mobile and easy to manage. For example, a virtual machine can be moved or copied from one location to another just like any other software file. In addition, a virtual machine can be stored on any standard storage medium, from a compact USB Flash memory stick to enterprise storage networks.

4   .Hardware Independence. Virtual machines are completely independent of the underlying physical hardware on which they run. For example, a virtual machine with virtual components (CPU, network card, SCSI controller) can be configured with settings that are completely different from the physical characteristics of the underlying hardware. Virtual machines can even run different operating systems (Windows, Linux, etc.) on the same physical server. Combined with the properties of encapsulation and compatibility, hardware independence provides the ability to freely move virtual machines from one x86-based computer to another without changing device drivers, OS or applications. Hardware independence also makes it possible to run completely different operating systems and applications in combination on the same physical computer.

Consider the main varieties of virtualisation, such as:

•   server virtualisation (full virtualisation and paravirtualisation) - virtualisation at the operating system level,

•   application virtualisation,

•   virtualisation of representations.

Server virtualisation

Today, when talking about virtualisation technologies, we usually mean server virtualisation, as the latter is becoming the most popular solution on the IT market. Server virtualisation implies running several virtual servers on one physical server. Virtual machines or servers are applications running on a host operating system that emulate the physical devices of the server. Each virtual machine may have an operating system on which applications and services can be installed. Typical representatives are VmWare (ESX, Server, Workstation) and Microsoft products (Hyper-V, Virtual Server, Virtual PC).

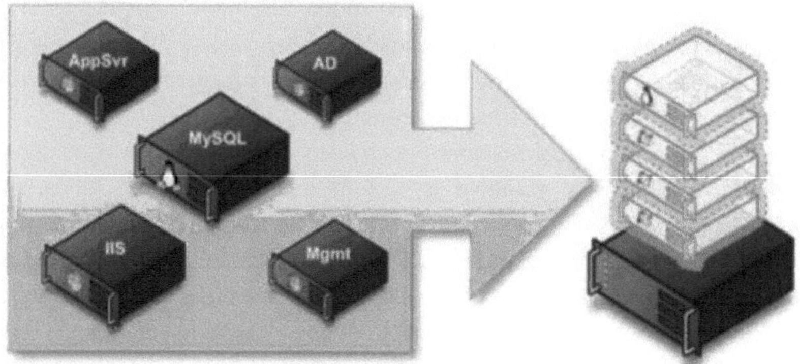

Figure 9.3. Server virtualisation

Data centres use a lot of space and a lot of energy, especially when you add in the accompanying cooling systems and infrastructure. Virtualisation technologies consolidate servers across a large number of physical servers into virtual machines on a single high-performance server.

The number of physical machines required to act as servers is reduced, which reduces the amount of energy required to run the machines and the space required to house them. A reduction in the number of servers and space reduces the amount of energy required to cool them. With less energy, less carbon dioxide is produced. This indicator, for example in Europe, is quite important.

An important factor is the financial side. Virtualisation is an important cost saving point. Virtualisation not only reduces the need to purchase additional physical servers, but also minimises the requirements for hosting them. The use of a virtual server offers advantages in terms of speed of deployment, utilisation and management, which reduces the waiting time for any project to be deployed.

Not so long ago, the latest generation of x86 processors from AMD and Intel appeared, where manufacturers added hardware virtualisation support for the first time. Prior to this, virtualisation was supported by software, which naturally resulted in high performance overheads.

For the personal computers that appeared in the eighties of the twentieth century, the problem of virtualisation of hardware resources seemed to be non-existent by definition, as each user had at his disposal the whole computer with its own operating system. But as PCs became more powerful and x86 systems became more widely used, the situation quickly changed. "Dialectical spiral" of development made its next turn, and at the turn of the century began another cycle of strengthening centripetal forces to concentrate computing resources. At the beginning of this decade, against the background of growing interest of enterprises in increasing the efficiency of their computer facilities, a new stage of virtualisation technologies development started, which is now mainly associated with the use of x86 architecture.

It should be noted that although there was nothing unknown in the ideas of x86-virtualisation in theoretical terms, it was a qualitatively new phenomenon for the IT-industry in comparison with the situation 20 years ago. The point is that in hardware and software architecture of mainframes and Unix-computers virtualisation issues were solved at once at the basic and hardware level. The x86 system was not built to work in data-centre mode at all, and its development in the direction of virtualisation is a rather complex evolutionary process with many different variants of solving the problem.

An important point also lies in qualitatively different business models of mainframe and x86 development. In the first case we are actually talking about a monovendor hardware and software complex to support a rather limited range of application software for a rather narrow range of large customers. In the second case, we are dealing with a decentralised community of hardware manufacturers, base software suppliers and a huge army of application software developers.

The use of x86 virtualisation tools started in the late 90s with workstations: while the number of client OS versions was increasing, the number of people (software developers, technical support specialists, experts) who needed to have several copies of different operating systems on one PC was constantly growing.

Virtualisation for server infrastructure started to be applied a little later, and it was connected, first of all, with the solution of tasks of consolidation of computing resources. But here two independent directions were formed at once:

-support for heterogeneous operating environments (including legacy applications). This case is most often encountered in corporate information systems. Technically, the problem is solved by simultaneous operation of several virtual machines on one computer, each of which includes an instance of the operating system. But this mode was implemented using two fundamentally different approaches: *full virtualisation* and *paravirtualisation*;

-support for homogeneous computing environments implies isolation of services within a single instance of an operating system kernel (OS-level virtualisation), which is most typical for application hosting by service providers. Of course, virtual machines can be used here as well, but it is much more efficient to create isolated containers based on a single OS kernel. The next life stage of x86 virtualisation technologies started in 2004-2006 and was connected with the beginning of their mass application in corporate systems. Accordingly, if earlier developers were mainly engaged in the creation of virtual environment execution technologies, now the tasks of managing these solutions and their integration into the general corporate IT infrastructure have come to the forefront. At the same time, there was a noticeable increase in demand for virtualisation on the part of personal users (but if in the 90s it was developers and testers, now we are talking about end users, both professional and home).

Many of the difficulties and challenges in developing virtualisation technologies are related to overcoming the legacy features of the x86 hardware and software architecture. There are several basic methods for this purpose:

Full, Native Virtualisation. It uses unmodified instances of guest operating systems, and to support these operating systems a common layer of emulation of their execution on top of the host operating system, which is a regular operating system. This technology is used in VMware Workstation, VMware Server (formerly GSX Server), Parallels Desktop, Parallels Server, MS Virtual PC, MS Virtual Server, and Virtual Iron, among others. The advantages of this approach include relative simplicity of implementation, versatility and reliability of the solution; all management functions are taken over by the host-OS. The disadvantages are high additional overhead costs for the hardware resources used, lack of consideration of guest OS peculiarities, less flexibility in the use of hardware than necessary.

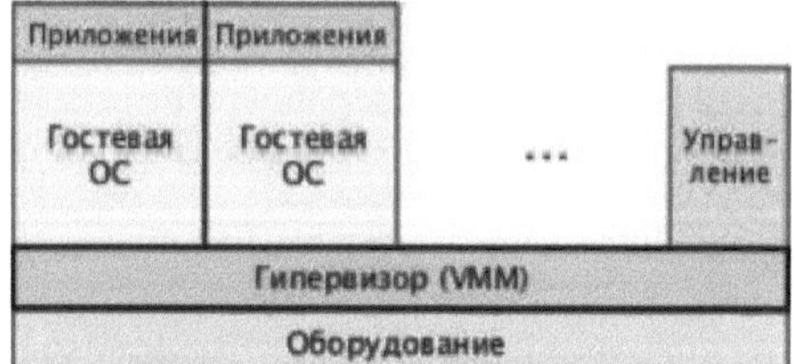

Figure 9.4. Full virtualisation

Paravirtualisation. Modification of the kernel of the guest OS is performed in such a way that it includes a new set of APIs through which it can work directly with the hardware without conflicting with other virtual machines. In this case, there is no need to use a full-fledged OS as host software, the functions of which in this case are performed by a special system called hypervisor. This variant is the most actual direction of development of server virtualisation technologies and is used in VMware ESX Server, Xen (and other vendors' solutions based on this technology), Microsoft Hyper-V. The advantages of this technology are in the absence of the need for a host OS - VMs are installed virtually on "bare hardware", and hardware resources are used efficiently. The disadvantages are the complexity of implementing the approach and the need to create a specialised hypervisor OS.

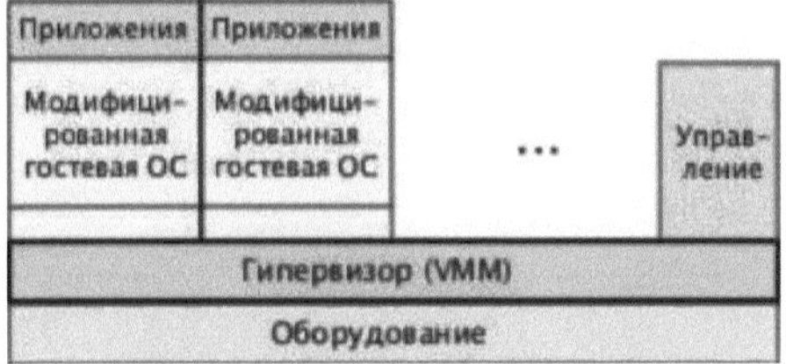

Figure 9.5. Paravirtualisation

Operating system-level virtualisation (operating system-level virtualisation). This option implies the use of a single kernel of the host OS to create independent parallel operating environments. For the guest software only its own network and hardware environment is created. This variant is used in Virtuozzo (for Linux and Windows), OpenVZ (free variant of Virtuozzo) and Solaris Containers. Advantages - high efficiency of hardware resources usage, low technical overheads, excellent manageability, minimised licensing costs. Disadvantages - implementation of only homogeneous computing environments.

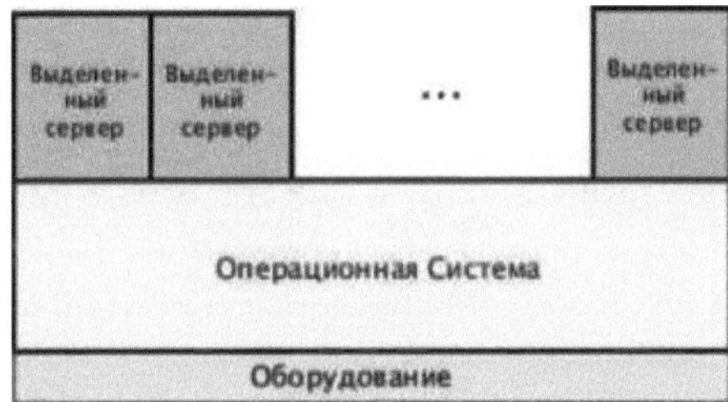

Figure 9.6. Virtualisation at the OS level

Application virtualisation implies the use of a model of strong isolation of application programs with controlled interaction with the OS, where each application instance, all its main components are virtualised: files (including system files), registry, fonts, INI-files, COM-objects, services. The application is executed without installation procedure in its traditional sense and can be launched directly from external media (e.g. flash cards or network folders). From an IT perspective, this approach has obvious advantages: faster desktop deployment and management, minimising not only conflicts between applications but also the need for compatibility testing. This technology allows multiple incompatible applications to be used on the same computer, or more precisely, on the same operating system at the same time. Application virtualisation allows users to run the same pre-configured application or group of applications from a server. The applications will run independently of each other without making any changes to the operating system. In fact, Sun Java Virtual Machine, Microsoft Application Virtualisation (previously called Softgrid), Thinstall (in early 2008 it became part of VMware), Symantec/Altiris all use this type of virtualisation.

Fig.9.7 Application virtualisation

Virtualisation of views (workspaces). View virtualisation implies emulation of the user interface. That is, the user sees the application and works with it on his terminal, although the application is actually running on a remote server, and the user receives only a picture of the remote application. Depending on the mode of operation, the user can see the remote desktop and the application running on it, or only the application window itself.

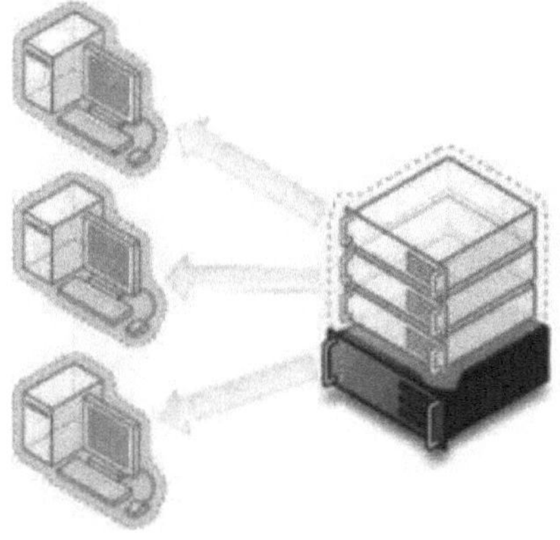

Business needs are changing the way we think about workflow organisation. The personal computer, which over the past decades has become an indispensable attribute of the office and a means of performing most office tasks, can no longer keep up with the growing needs of business. The real tool of the user turns out to be software, which is only attached to the PC, making it an intermediate link of the corporate information system. As a result, cloud computing, where users have access to their own data but do not manage or think about the infrastructure, operating system and the actual software they work with, is actively developing.

However, with the growing scale of organisations, the use of user PCs in IT infrastructure is causing a number of challenges:

- high operating costs to support the computer fleet;
- The complexity associated with managing desktop PCs;
- Ensuring that users have safe and secure access to the software and applications they need to work;
- technical support for users;
- installation and renewal of software licences and maintenance;
- backup, etc.

To avoid these complexities and reduce the costs associated with solving them, it is possible to use Virtual Desktop Infrastructure (VDI) technology to virtualise employee workstations. VDI allows to separate the user software from the hardware - the personal computer - and access client applications through terminal devices.

VDI is a combination of remote desktop connections and virtualisation. The serving servers run multiple virtual machines, with client operating systems such as Windows 7, Windows Vista and Windows XP or Linux operating systems. Users remotely connect to the virtual machine of their desktop environment. On users' local computers, terminal clients, legacy hardware with Microsoft Windows Fundamentals or a Linux distribution can be used as a remote desktop client.

VDI completely isolates the users' virtual environment from other virtual environments, as each user connects to a separate virtual machine. Sometimes a static VDI infrastructure is used where the user always connects to the same virtual machine, other times dynamic VDI where users dynamically connect to different virtual machines and virtual machines are created as needed. With either model, it is important to keep user data out of virtual machines and quickly provision applications.

Along with centralised management and easy provisioning of computers, VDI provides access to the desktop environment from anywhere, as long as users can remotely connect to the server.

Let's imagine that there is a problem on a client computer. You have to run diagnostics and possibly reinstall the operating system. With VDI, in the event of a malfunction, you can simply delete the virtual machine and create a new environment in seconds using a pre-created virtual machine template. VDI provides additional security because data is not stored locally on a desktop or laptop.

As an example of virtualisation of views, we can also consider thin terminal technology, which actually virtualises the workplaces of desktop system users: the user is not bound to a particular PC, but can access his files and applications, which are located on the server, from any remote terminal after performing the authorisation procedure. All user commands and the session image on the monitor are emulated by the thin client management software. The use of this technology makes it possible to centralise the maintenance of client workstations and drastically reduce their support costs - for example, to upgrade to the next version of a client application, new software only needs to be installed once on the server.

One of the most famous thin clients is the Sun Ray terminal, which uses Sun Ray Server Software to organise its operation. To start a Sun Ray session it is enough to insert an identification smart card into this device. The use of a smart card significantly increases the mobility of the user - he can move from one Sun Ray to another by moving his card between them and immediately continue working with his applications from where he left off at the previous terminal. And abandoning the hard drive not only ensures user mobility and improves data security, but also significantly reduces power consumption compared to conventional PCs, so the Sun terminal has no fan and runs virtually silent. In addition, reducing the number of components of the thin terminal also reduces the risk of failure, and therefore saves maintenance costs. Another advantage of the Sun Ray is a significantly extended product life cycle compared to conventional PCs, as there are no components that can become obsolete.

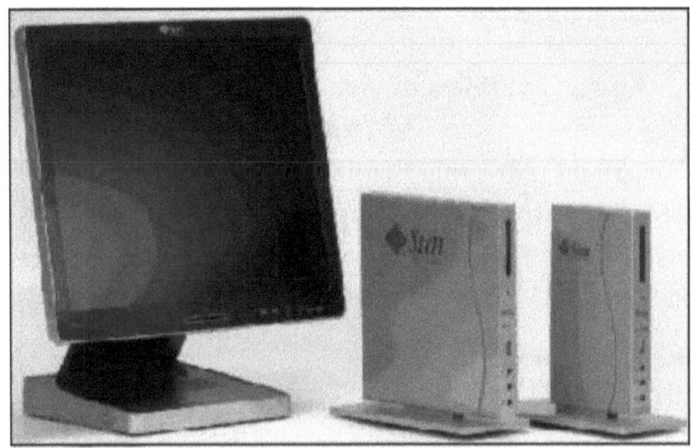

Figure 9.9. An example of a thin client. Sun Ray terminal.

A brief overview of virtualisation platforms
VMware

VMware is one of the early players in the virtualisation platform market. VMware patented its virtualisation software techniques in 1998 and since then has released many efficient and professional virtualisation products at various levels, from VMware Workstation, designed for desktop PCs, to VMware ESX Server, which allows consolidation of physical enterprise servers in a virtual infrastructure.

Unlike mainframe computers, x86-based devices do not fully support virtualisation. Therefore, VMware has had to overcome many challenges in creating virtual machines for x86-based computers. The primary function of most CPUs (in computers and PCs) is to execute a sequence of stored instructions (i.e., programmes). The x86 based CPUs contain 17 specific instructions that cause problems with virtualisation, causing the operating system to display a warning message, interrupt an application, or just give a general failure. So, these 17 instructions proved to be a significant obstacle in the initial implementation of virtualisation for x86-based computers.

To overcome this obstacle, VMware has developed adaptive virtualisation technology that "intercepts" these instructions at the creation stage and converts them into secure instructions suitable for virtualisation without affecting the execution of all other instructions. The result is a high-performance virtual machine that matches the host hardware and maintains full software compatibility. VMware was the first to develop and deploy this innovative technology, making it the undisputed leader in virtualisation technology today.

VMware's extensive list of products includes many tools to improve efficiency and optimise IT infrastructure, manage virtual servers, and migrate from physical to virtual platforms. According to various performance tests, VMware virtualisation tools almost always beat the competition on most parameters. VMware has more than 100,000 customers worldwide, with 100% of Fortune 100 organisations on its customer list. Its network of partnerships includes more than 350 hardware and software vendors and more than 6,000 resellers. VMware's market share is currently estimated at 80 per cent. Meanwhile, among virtualisation platforms, VMware has a lot to choose from:

VMware Workstation is a desktop-oriented platform designed for use by software developers and IT professionals. A new version of the popular VMware Workstation 7 product became available in 2009, supporting

Windows and Linux as host operating systems. VMware Workstation 7 can be used in conjunction with a development environment, making it particularly popular with developers, educators and technical support professionals. The release of VMware Workstation 7 signifies official support for Windows 7 as both a guest and host operating system. The product includes support for Aero Peek and Flip 3D, which makes it possible to view a virtual machine by moving the cursor to the VMware taskbar or the corresponding tab on the host desktop. The new version can run on any version of Windows 7, just as any version of Windows can be run in virtual machines. In addition, virtual machines in VMware Workstation 7, fully support the Windows Display Driver

Model (WDDM), which allows the Windows Aero interface to be used in guest machines.

VMware Player is a free virtual machine "player" based on VMware Workstation virtual machine, designed to run ready-made virtual machine images created in other VMware products, as well as in Microsoft VirtualPC and Symantec LiveState Recovery. As of version 3.0, VMware Player also allows you to create virtual machine images. The limited functionality now mainly concerns functions intended for IT specialists and software developers.

VMware Fusion is Apple's desktop virtualisation product for the Mac platform.

VMware Server, Free Product VMware Server is a fairly powerful virtualisation platform that can be run on servers running Windows and Linux host operating systems. The main purpose of VMware Server is to support small and medium-sized virtual infrastructures of small businesses. Due to its low complexity of mastering and installation, VMware Server can be deployed in the shortest possible time, both on the servers of organisations and on the computers of home users.

VMware Ace is a product for creating security policy-protected virtual machines that can then be distributed via a Software-as-a-Service (SaaS) model.

VMware vSphere is a suite of products that provides a robust platform for data centre virtualisation. The company also positions the suite as a powerful virtualisation platform for building and deploying a private cloud. VMware vSphere comes in several editions with features specifically designed for small businesses and mid-sized companies and corporations.

VMware vSphere includes a number of components that transform standard hardware into an overall resilient, mainframe-like environment that includes built-in service level controls for all applications:

• Infrastructure Services are components that provide comprehensive virtualisation of server, storage and network resources, aggregating them and accurately allocating them to applications on demand and in line with business priorities.

• Application Services are components that provide built-in service level controls for all applications on the vSphere Platform platform, regardless of their type or OS.

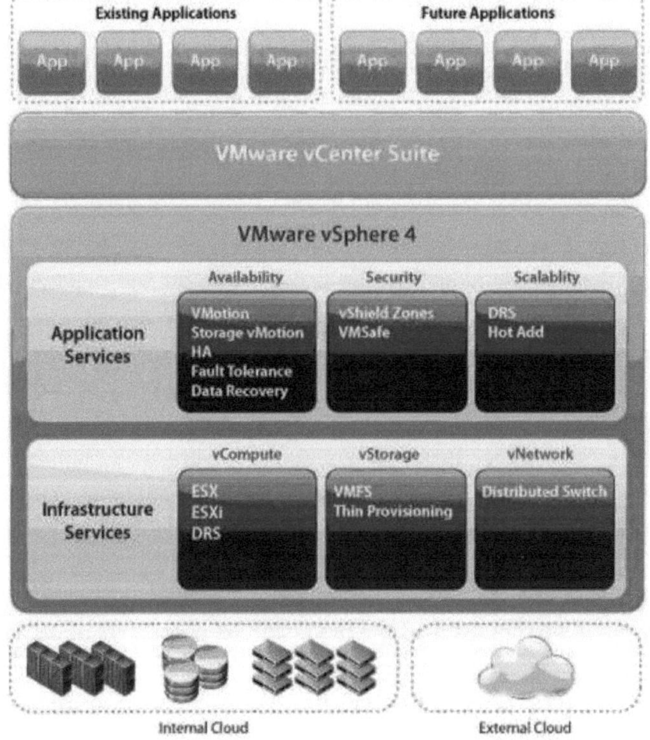

Figure 10.1: Structure of the vShpere platform.

• VMware vCenter Server provides a central virtualisation management console for administration of infrastructure and application services. This console supports comprehensive visibility into all aspects of your virtual infrastructure, automating day-to-day operations and scalability for managing large data centre environments.

VMware ESX Server is a hypervisor that partitions physical servers into multiple virtual machines. VMware ESX is the foundation of the VMware vSphere suite and is included in all releases of VMware vSphere.

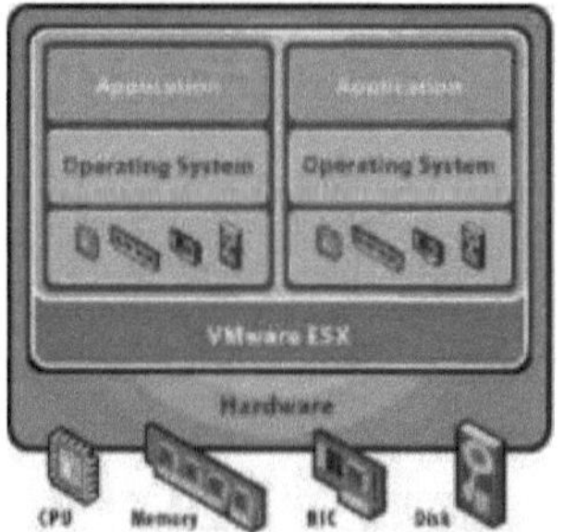

Figure 10.2: VMware ESX hypervisor.

VMware vSphere Hypervisor (formerly VMware ESXi) is a "lightweight" enterprise virtualisation platform based on ESX technologies. The product is free and available for download from the VMware website. VSphere VMware Hypervisor is the easiest way to get started with virtualisation

VMware vCenter - provides an extensible and scalable platform to proactively manage your virtual infrastructure and deliver comprehensive information about it. VMware vCenter Server provides centralised management of vSphere environments and simplifies day-to-day tasks, dramatically improving the administration of your environment. It provides extensive server consolidation, configuration, and management capabilities. VMware vCenter Server aggregates all aspects of virtual environment management, from virtual machines to gathering information about physical servers for migration to virtual infrastructure. In addition to the central virtual infrastructure management product vCenter Server, there are also a number of add-ons that implement various aspects of planning, management and integration of distributed virtual infrastructure (VMware vCenter Server Heartbeat, VMware vCenter Orchestrator, VMware vCenter Capacity IQ, VMware vCenter Site Recovery Manager, VMware vCenter Lab Manager, VMware vCenter Configuration Manager, VMware vCenter Converter). In particular, vCenter Converter is designed to migrate physical servers to a virtual environment, allowing for "hot" (without system shutdown) and "cold" migration. vCenter Site Recovery Manager is software for creating a geographically remote backup segment of the virtual infrastructure, which, in the event of failure of the main node, takes over the functions of running virtual machines in accordance with the disaster recovery plan. vCenter Lab Manager is a product for creating an infrastructure for storing and delivering virtual machine configurations, enabling an efficient testing scheme in software development companies.

VMware ThinApp is a former product of Thinstall Virtualisation Suite, an application virtualisation software   that   allows you to distribute pre-installed applications on client workstations, reducing the time spent on standard installation and configuration operations.

VMware View is a suite of products that centralises user desktops in virtual machines on the vSphere platform. This reduces the cost of standard IT operations associated with deploying and maintaining user desktops.

VMware Capacity Planner is a tool that centrally collects and analyses server hardware, software, and hardware performance data. This data is used by authorised VMware partners to build consolidation plans for virtual machines on the VMware ESX Server platform.

VMware VMmark is a hardware vendor-only product designed to test the performance of VMware ESX Server on server platforms.

Citrix (Xen)

The development of the Xen non-commercial hypervisor began as a research project at the University of Cambridge Computer Laboratory. The project's founder and leader was Ian Pratt of the university, who went on to found XenSource, a company dedicated to developing commercial virtualisation platforms based on the Xen hypervisor, as well as supporting the Open Source community for the Xen non-commercial product. Xen was originally the most advanced platform to support paravirtualisation technology. This technology allows a hypervisor on a host system to control a guest OS via VMI (Virtual Machine Interface) hypercalls, which requires modification of the guest system kernel. Currently, a free version of Xen is included in the distributions of several operating systems such as Red Hat, Novell SUSE, Debian, Fedora Core, and Sun Solaris. In mid-August 2007, XenSource was acquired by Citrix Systems. The amount of the deal is about $500 million (in shares and cash), which indicates Citrix's serious intentions regarding virtualisation. Experts believe that the purchase of Citrix by Microsoft is not excluded, given its long-standing co-operation with XenSource.

Free Xen. Currently, the Open Source version of the Xen platform is mainly used for educational and research purposes. Some successful ideas implemented by numerous developers from all over the world are reflected in commercial versions of Citrix virtualisation products. Free versions of Xen are now included with many Linux systems, allowing users to use virtual machines to isolate software in guest operating systems for testing and security studies, without having to install a virtualisation platform. In addition, many independent software developers can distribute software using virtual templates that already have the guest system and product offering installed and configured. In addition, Xen is ideal for maintaining legacy software in a virtual machine. For more serious enterprise production environments, however, Citrix commercial platforms should be used.

Citrix XenApp is designed to virtualise and publish applications to optimise the service delivery infrastructure of large enterprises. XenApp has a huge global user base and is a key component of the IT infrastructure in many companies.

Citrix XenServer is a medium-sized enterprise server consolidation platform that includes basic capabilities for maintaining virtual infrastructure. The manufacturer positions this product as an Enterprise-level solution for server virtualisation that supports work in a cloud environment.

Citrix XenDesktop is an enterprise desktop virtualisation solution that enables centralised storage and delivery of desktop environments in virtual machines to users. The product supports multiple application delivery scenarios across desktops, thin clients and mobile PCs and is compatible with competitors' server virtualisation solutions.

Microsoft

For Microsoft, it all started when in 2003 it acquired Connectix, one of the few companies producing virtualisation software for Windows. Along with Connectix, Microsoft got Virtual PC, which at the time was competing with VMware's desktop virtualisation solutions. By and large, Virtual PC provided the same number of features as VMware Workstation, and with proper attention, could be a full-fledged competitor to that platform today. However, since that time, Microsoft has been releasing a minor release a year, with little focus on Virtual PC, while VMware has been rapidly developing its virtualisation system into a truly professional tool. Realising its technological lag in the virtualisation of server platforms, Microsoft released Virtual Server 2005, aimed at creating and consolidating virtual servers for organisations. However, it was too late. VMware had already seized leadership in this market segment, offering two server virtualisation platforms at the time, VMware GSX Server and VMware ESX Server, each of which was superior to Microsoft's platform in many ways. The final blow came in 2006, when VMware effectively declared the VMware GSX Server product free, taking over the development of the VMware Server product based on it and concentrating all its efforts on selling the powerful VMware ESX Server enterprise platform as part of Virtual Infrastructure 3. Microsoft had only one way out in this situation: in April 2006, it also announced the free product Microsoft Virtual Server 2005. Also, the previously existing two editions Standard Edition and Enterprise Edition were merged into one - Microsoft

Virtual Server Enterprise Edition. Since then Microsoft has significantly changed its virtualisation strategy and in the summer of 2008 the final release of the Microsoft Hyper-V virtualisation platform was released, integrated into Windows Server 2008. The virtualisation server role is now available to all users of Microsoft's new server operating system.

Microsoft Virtual Server. Microsoft Virtual Server virtualisation platform can be used on a server running Windows Server 2003 operating system and is designed to run several virtual machines simultaneously on one physical host. The platform is free of charge and provides only basic functions.

Microsoft Virtual PC. The Virtual PC product was purchased by Microsoft Corporation along with Connectix and was first released under the Microsoft brand as Microsoft Virtual PC 2004. In acquiring Virtual PC and Connectix, Microsoft had far-reaching plans to provide users with a tool to facilitate migration to the next version of the Windows operating system. Virtual PC 2007 is now free and available to support desktop operating systems in virtual machines.

Microsoft Hyper-V. Microsoft's product is positioned as the main competitor to VMware ESX Server in the field of enterprise virtualisation platforms. Microsoft Hyper-V is a solution for virtualisation of servers based on processors with x64 architecture in corporate environments. Unlike Microsoft Virtual Server or Virtual PC products, Hyper-V provides virtualisation at the hardware level, using virtualisation technologies embedded in processors. Hyper-V provides high performance, almost equal to that of a single operating system running on a dedicated server. Hyper-V is distributed in two ways: as part of Windows Server 2008 or as part of Microsoft's independent, free Hyper-V Server product.

With Windows Server 2008, Hyper-V technology can be deployed in either a full installation or in Server Core mode, with Hyper-V Server running in Core mode only. This allows you to fully realise all the benefits of a thin, cost-effective and manageable virtualisation platform.

Hyper-V is a built-in component of the 64-bit versions of Win- dows Server 2008 Standard, Windows Server 2008 Enterprise, and Windows Server 2008 Datacenter. This technology is not available in 32-bit versions of Windows Server 2008, Windows Server 2008 Standard without Hyper-V, Windows Server 2008 Enterprise without Hyper-V, Windows Server 2008 Datacenter without Hyper-V, Windows Web Server 2008, and Windows Server 2008 for Itanium-based systems.

Figure 10.3: Virtualisation architecture with hypervisor

Hyper-v is a hypervisor, i.e. a layer between the hardware and virtual machines below the operating system. This architecture was originally developed by IBM in the 1960s for mainframes and has recently become available on x86/x64 platforms as part of a number of solutions including Windows Server 2008 Hyper-V and Vmware ESX.

Hypervisor-based virtualisation is based on the fact that there is a layer between the hardware and virtual machines that intercepts operating system access to the processor, memory and other devices. Access to peripherals can be organised differently in different hypervisor implementations. In terms of existing solutions for implementing the virtual machine manager, we can distinguish two main types of hypervisor architecture: microkernel and monolithic.

The monolithic approach places the hypervisor in a single tier that also includes most of the required components such as the kernel, device drivers, and I/O stack. This is the approach used by solutions such as VMware ESX and traditional mainframe systems.

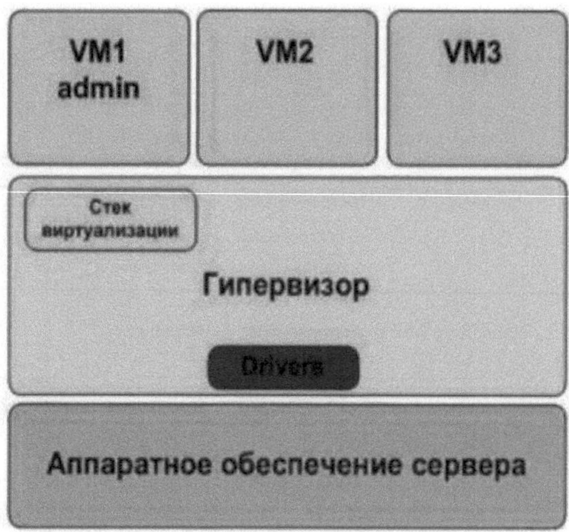

Figure 10.4: Architecture of a monolithic hypervisor

The monolithic approach implies that all device drivers are placed in the hypervisor. In the monolithic model, the hypervisor uses its own drivers to access hardware. Guest operating systems run in virtual machines on top of the hypervisor. When a guest system needs access to hardware, it must go through the hypervisor and its driver model. Typically, one of the guest OSes plays the role of an administrator or console that runs components to provision, manage, and monitor all guest OSes running on the server.

The monolithic hypervisor model provides excellent performance but has a number of drawbacks such as:

•   Resilience - if a bug gets into the updated version of the driver, the result will be failures in the whole system, in all its virtual machines.

•   Driver update issues - if you need to update the driver of a device (for example, a network adapter), you can only update the driver when a new version of the hypervisor is released that will integrate the new driver for that device.

•   Difficulties using unsupported hardware. For example, you intend to use hardware "Server" powerful and reliable enough, but at the same time the hypervisor does not have the necessary driver for RAID controller or network adapter. This will make it impossible to use the corresponding hardware, and thus the server.

The microkernel approach uses a very thin, specialised hypervisor that performs only the basic tasks of providing partition isolation and memory management. This layer does not include the I/O stack or device drivers. This is the approach used by Hyper V. In this architecture, the virtualisation stack and specific device drivers are located in a dedicated OS partition called the parent partition.

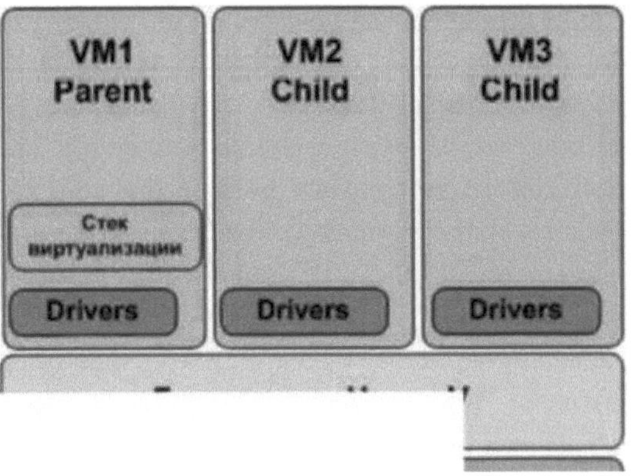

Hyper-V hypervisor

Server hardware

Figure 10.5: Microkernel hypervisor architecture

In a microkernel implementation, you can talk about a "thin hypervisor", in which case there are no drivers in the hypervisor at all. Instead, drivers run in each individual partition so that any guest OS can access the hardware through the hypervisor. With this arrangement, each virtual machine occupies a completely separate partition, which has a positive impact on security and reliability. In the microkernel model of the hypervisor (which is the model used in Windows Server 2008 R2 virtualisation), one partition is a parent and the rest are children. A partition is the smallest isolated unit supported by the hypervisor. The Hyper-V hypervisor is less than 1.5 MB in size and can fit on a single 3.5-inch floppy disk.

Each partition is assigned specific hardware resources, such as a share of CPU time, memory, devices, etc. The parent partition creates and manages child partitions and contains the virtualisation stack used to manage the child partitions. The parent partition is created first and owns all resources not owned by the hypervisor. Having all hardware resources means that it is the root (i.e. parent) partition that manages power, connects self-configuring devices, handles hardware failures, and even manages hypervisor booting.

The parent partition contains the virtualisation stack, which is a set of software components that sit on top of the hypervisor and work together to provide virtual machines. The virtualisation stack communicates with the hypervisor and performs all virtualisation functions not directly supported by the hypervisor. Most of these functions are related to the creation and management of child partitions and the resources (CPU, memory, devices) they require.

The advantage of the microkernel approach used in Windows Server 2008 R2 over the monolithic approach is that the drivers that must reside between the parent partition and the physical server do not require any changes to the driver model. In other words, existing drivers can simply be applied to the system. Microsoft chose this approach because the need to develop new drivers would have severely slowed down the development of the system. As for guest operating systems, they will work with emulators or synthetic devices.

On the other hand, a microkernel model may lose slightly to a monolithic model in performance. However, security has become a top priority these days, so for most companies it is quite acceptable to lose a couple of per cent in performance for the sake of reducing the attack front and increasing resilience.

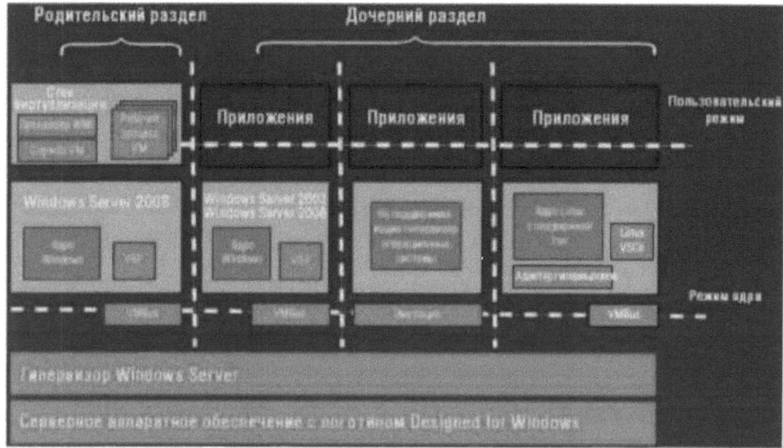

Figure 10.6: Hyper-v architecture

All versions of Hyper-V have a single parent partition. This partition manages Hyper-V features. The Windows Server Virtualisation console runs from the parent partition. In addition, the parent partition is used to run virtual machines (VMs) that support streaming emulation of legacy hardware. These VMs, built on off-the-shelf templates that emulate hardware, are analogous to VMs running in host-based virtualisation products such as Virtual Server.

Guest VMs run from Hyper-V child partitions. Child partitions support two types of VMs: high-performance VMs based on VMBus architecture and VMs managed by the host system. The first group includes VMs running

Windows Server 2003, Windows Vista, Server 2008, and Linux (supporting Xen). The new VMBus architecture features a high-performance pipeline that operates in RAM, connecting Virtualisation Service Clients (VSCs) on guest VMs to the host's Virtual Service Provider (VSP). Host-managed VMs run platforms that do not support the new VMBus architecture: Windows NT, Windows 2000, and Linux (without Xen technology support, such as SUSE Linux Server Enterprise 10).

Microsoft System Center Virtual Machine Manager (SCVMM) is a standalone product in the System Center family for managing virtual infrastructure, efficiently using the resources of physical hosts, and simplifying the preparation and creation of new guest systems for administrators and users. The product provides comprehensive support for consolidating physical servers in a virtual infrastructure, fast and reliable conversion of physical machines into virtual machines, intelligent placement of virtual workloads on suitable physical nodes, and a single console for resource management and optimisation. SCVMM provides the following capabilities:

• Centralised management of virtual machine servers across the enterprise. SCVMM supports management of Microsoft Hyper-V, Microsoft Virtual Server, VMware ESX servers and future support for Xen.

• Create a library of virtual machine templates. Virtual machine templates are sets of pre-installed operating system images that can be deployed in minutes.

• Monitor and place virtual machines to match the workload of physical servers.

• Migration (conversion) of physical servers to virtual machines - P2V technology. P2V technology allows you to migrate a physical server to a virtual server without stopping work. Thus, there is a possibility of online backup of the whole server, and in case of its failure, it is possible to start the virtual server within a minute and continue working.

• Migration (conversion) of virtual machines of other formats to Hyper-V virtual machines - V2V technology. This technology is similar to P2V, but allows you to migrate Microsoft Virtual Server or VMware ESX virtual machines to Hyper-V.

• Hyper-V cluster management.

Key differences between cloud technology and virtualisation

By table, the difference between cloud computing and virtualisation will be more evident.

Parameter	Cloud computing	Virtualisation

	Unlimited, can be extended indefinitely	Limited to virtual hardware configuration
Scalability		
Installation speed	The procedure is lengthy, labour-intensive	Simple, quick setup, requires minimum knowledge
Flexible settings	High: a user can access their cloud from any corner of the world and gadget, provided they have an internet connection	To get access to the virtual machine you need to go authentication
Type of service	IaaS	SaaS
Required equipment	Requires multiple hardware to enable cloud computing	Each virtual machine requires its own hardware
Integration capability	Anticipates future expansion: adding more applications, users	Within the same infrastructure, allows you to add new devices
Dependence	The same link on the network can be accessed by multiple users, including simultaneously	Multiple operating systems can be installed on the same computer/server
Accessibility	Broad: any user with internet access	Low: access only to those connected to the network. Third party users can only gain access through authorisation
Disaster recovery	If one of the machines goes down, the cloud will continue to run, distributing its load to the other hardware	Failures in one machine can cause other virtual appliances to fail
Possible types	Public and private cloud	Hardware virtualisation and application virtualisation

Summary of results:

Despite these differences, cloud technology and virtualisation are closely related. And cloud infrastructure cannot be built without virtualisation. Virtualisation is responsible for taking the hardware out of the physical PC. It is used to create multiple virtual machines on a single server. Cloud, on the other hand, uses these infrastructures, combines multiple programmes, applications to create separate instances for all users.

During this lecture we got acquainted with virtualisation technologies, considered the main types of virtualisation. We also considered a set of software products of the largest virtualisation companies

Key Terms:

Virtualisation is the process of presenting a set of computational resources or their logical aggregation that gives any advantages over the original configuration.

A virtual machine is a software or hardware environment that hides the real implementation of a process or object from its visible representation.

Full Virtualisation - Virtualisation where unmodified instances of guest operating systems are used, and to support the operation of these operating systems a common layer of emulation of their execution on top of the host operating system, which is a regular operating system.

Paravirtualisation - Virtualisation where the kernel of the guest OS is modified to include a new set of APIs through which it can work directly with the hardware without conflicting with other virtual machines.

OS-level virtualisation - A type of virtualisation that involves using a single host OS kernel to create independent parallel operating environments.

Server virtualisation is the running of multiple virtual servers on a single physical server. Virtual machines or servers are applications running on a host operating system that emulate the physical devices of the server. Each virtual machine can have an operating system on which applications and services can be installed.

Application virtualisation is a type of virtualisation that implies application of a model of strong isolation of application programs with controlled interaction with the OS, where each application instance, all its main components are virtualised: files (including system files), registry, fonts, INI-files, COM-objects, services. The application is executed without the installation procedure in its traditional sense and can be launched directly from external media.

Virtualisation of views (jobs)

View virtualisation takes place when a server makes its resources available to clients, with the client application running on that server and the client receiving only the view.

Monolithic hypervisor architecture - A hypervisor architecture in which the hypervisor is hosted in a single layer that also includes most of the required components such as the kernel, device drivers, and I/O stack

Microkernel hypervisor architecture - An approach that uses a very thin, specialised hypervisor that performs only the basic tasks of providing partition isolation and memory management. This layer does not include an I/O stack or device drivers.

Platform Overview
The most common cloud platforms

The most common cloud platforms are summarised in Table 11.1.

Table 11.1: Most common cloud platforms

Platforms Ha r a kter i stics'.	Amazon Web Services	Google Arr Engine	Microsoft Windows Azure
Type	laaS	PaaS	PaaS
Developed services	Computing services, storage services	Web applications	Web applications and non-Web applications
Virtualisation	OS layer, with the Hep hypervisor running	Application container	OS level
User access interface	Console utilities Amazon EU2.	Web-based administration console	Microsoft Portal Windows Azure
Web APIs	Yes	Yes	Yes
Development environment	Absent	Python, Java	Microsoft .NET

Amazon Web Services

***Amazon Web Services (AWS) is a* set of web-based computing services that make up the cloud computing platform introduced by Amazon in early 2006**. The most well-known services are *Amazon EC2* and *Amazon S3*. This infrastructure includes services for providing various services such as: data storage (file hosting, distributed data storage), virtual server leasing, provisioning of computing power, etc.

Figure 11.1: Amazon Web Services Architecture

Amazon Web Services Cloud *Services*:
- ***Amazon AWS*** Authentication - authenticate access to various services.

- *Amazon CloudFront is a* content delivery network (CDN) for delivering objects to near-demand locations.
- *Amazon CloudWatch* provides monitoring of *AWS* cloud resources and applications, starting with *EC2*.
- *Amazon DevPay is a* billing system (a system for billing customers for services provided by a company and goods sold*)* and account management system for applications that are built on *Amazon* Web Services.
- *Amazon Elastic Beanstalk* enables rapid deployment and management of applications *in* the cloud.
- *Amazon Elastic Block Store (EBS)* provides persistent storage volumes for *EC2*.
- *Amazon Elastic Compute Cloud (EC2)* provides scalable virtual private servers using *Xen*.
- *Amazon Elastic MapReduce* enables enterprises, researchers, analysts, and developers to easily and cheaply process large amounts of data. It uses the Hadoop framework running on EC2 and Amazon S3 web scalable infrastructure.
- *Amazon ElastiCache* provides in-memory caching for web applications.
- *Amazon Flexible Payments Service (FPS)* provides an interface for micropayments.
- *Amazon Fulfillment Web* Service provides a software web service for sellers to upload items to and from Amazon using the Fulfillment service.
- *Amazon Glacier* provides low cost storage based on the S3 storage solution.
- *Amazon Mechanical Turk (Mturk)* manages small units of work distributed among many people.
- *Amazon Product Advertising API* formerly known as Amazon Associates Web Service (A2S) and Amazon E-Commerce Service (ECS), provides access to Amazon product data and e-commerce functionality.
- *Amazon Relational Database Service (RDS)* provides a scalable database server with support for MySQL and Oracle.
- *Amazon Route 53* ensures the availability and scalability of the Domain Name System (DNS).
- *Amazon CloudSearch* provides basic full text search and indexing of text content.
- *Amazon Simple Service Email (SES)* provides email sending.
- *Amazon Simple Storage Service (S3)* provides a web-based storage service.
- *Amazon Simple Service Queue (SQS)* provides message queuing for web

applications.

• ***Amazon Simple Service Notification (SNS)*** provides a multi-protocol message push for a web application.

• ***Amazon Simple Workflow (SWF)*** *is a* service for building scalable, resilient applications.

• ***Amazon SimpleDB*** allows developers to query structured data. It works in conjunction with EC2 and S3 to provide "basic database functionality."

• ***Amazon Virtual Private Cloud (VPC)*** creates a logically federated set of Amazon EC2 elements that can be connected to an existing network using a VPN connection.

• ***AWS CloudFormation*** builds a set of related AWS resources and delivers them in an organised and predictable way.

• ***AWS Import. Export*** accelerates the movement of large amounts of data to and from AWS using portable storage devices.

• ***AWS Management Console (AWS Console)*** *is a* console for managing and monitoring *Amazon's* infrastructure, including *EC2, EBS, Amazon* Elastic MapReduce, Amazon CloudFront.

• ***AWS Storage Gateway*** *is an* ISCSI protocol storage appliance that supports cloud backup.

As you can see, AWS consists of a variety of cloud services that can be used in combinations to meet your business requirements and organisational objectives. To access these services, you can use the AWS management console, command line interface, or development kits (SDKs).

AWS Management Console

Access and manage Amazon Web Services through the AWS9 Management Console, a simple and intuitive user interface. You can also use the AWS Console mobile app to quickly browse resources on the go.

AWS command line interface

The AWS Command Line Interface is a single tool for managing your AWS services. By downloading just one tool, you can control multiple AWS services from the command line and automate them with scripts.

SDK packages

Our development kits (SDKs) make it easy to use AWS services in your applications with an application programming interface tailored to the programming language or platform you use.

Amazon Elastic Compute Cloud (Amazon EC2)

Amazon Elastic Compute Cloud (Amazon EC2) is a web service that provides computing power in the cloud. The service is part of the *Amazon Web Services* infrastructure. This system simplifies Internet computing for developers.

Amazon EC2's simple web services interface allows you to get and configure resources with minimal effort. It gives users full control over the resources they can run in Amazon's proven computing environment. Using Amazon EC2, you can get and load new server instances (Amazon EC2 instances, instance instances) in minutes to quickly scale resources in any direction as your needs change. Amazon EC2 changes the economics of computing by providing the ability to pay only for the resources used. Amazon EC2 gives developers and system administrators the tools to build fault-tolerant applications and protect against common failure scenarios.

At the core of Amazon Web Services is Amazon Elastic Compute Cloud (Amazon EC2) together with storage services. EC2 provides the user with a choice of virtual machines that can be run in a distributed computing environment. A virtual machine (called Amazon Machine Image - AMI) can be based on virtually any operating system (various versions of Windows and Linux distributions) and can work with any software infrastructure (MySQL, Oracle, etc.).

With *EC2* you can:

• Create an *Amazon Machine Image (AMI)* that contains applications, libraries, data, and associated configuration settings. Or use customised image templates to get the job done;

• upload AMIs to *Amazon S3. Amazon EC2* provides tools, for storing AMIs. *Amazon S3* provides secure, reliable, and fast storage for storing images;

• Use *Amazon EC2.* Web service for configuring security and network access;

• select operating system type(s), start, terminate, or monitor multiple *AMIs* as needed using the webservice *API*, or the various management tools that are provided;

• Determine the need to work in multiple locations, use static *IP* or other options;

• to pay only for the resources you need.

Advantages

Elastic computing resources at the scale of the Internet

Amazon EC2 allows you to increase or decrease processing power in minutes, not hours or days. You can commission a single server instance, hundreds or even thousands of server instances at the same time. And because all of these processes are managed by web service APIs, the application can automatically scale in any direction based on current needs.

Full control

You retain full control over your Amazon EC2 instances. You have administrative access to each instance and can interact with them like normal machines. You can stop your Amazon EC2 instances by saving data in the boot section and later restart the same instance using the web service API. Instances can be remotely restarted using the Web services API.

Flexible cloud hosting services

You can choose from a variety of instance types, operating systems, and software packages. Amazon EC2 allows you to choose the optimal memory configuration, CPU, instance storage, and boot partition size for your operating systems and applications. For example, you can choose from numerous Linux and Microsoft Windows Server distributions.

Integration

Amazon EC2 is integrated with most AWS services such as Amazon Simple Storage Service (Amazon S3), Amazon Relational Database Service (Amazon RDS), and Amazon Virtual Private Cloud (Amazon VPC), forming a full-featured, secure compute, query, and cloud storage solution for a variety of applications.

Reliability

Amazon EC2 offers a highly reliable environment where new instances can be brought online quickly. The service is powered by Amazon's proven network infrastructure and data centre. Under a Service Level Agreement (SLA), the company is committed to ensuring 99.95 per cent availability of the Amazon EC2 service in each region.

Safety

Amazon EC2 along with Amazon VPC provide secure and reliable networking features for computing resources.

☐ Your compute instances are located in a VPC in the IP address range you specify. You decide which instances will have access to the Internet and which will remain isolated.

☐ Using security groups and access control lists, you can control inbound and outbound network access to and from your instances.

☐ You can connect your existing IT infrastructure to resources in your VPC virtual cloud using IPsec VPN connections with standard encryption.

☐ Amazon EC2 resources can be prepared to run as dedicated instances. Dedicated instances are Amazon EC2 instances that run on hardware that is dedicated for use by a single client, which provides additional isolation.

☐ You can prepare your Amazon EC2 resources on dedicated hosts - physical servers with EC2 resources dedicated exclusively for your use.

Dedicated hosts can help meet compliance requirements and reduce costs by allowing you to use existing server software licences.

Low price

Amazon EC2 provides the financial benefits that come from running a large-scale computing infrastructure. You only pay for the computing resources used at a very favourable price.

☐ **On-demand instances** provide the option to pay hourly for the amount of computing resources without long-term commitments. Depending on application needs, computing resources can be increased or decreased, paying only for the instances in use at a specified hourly rate. The use of on-demand instances eliminates the cost and complexity of planning, purchasing and maintaining hardware and allows you to transform large capital expenditures into significantly lower variable costs. Moreover, by choosing on-demand instances, you do not need to purchase resources in reserve to cope with periodic traffic peaks.

☐ **Reserved Instances** - Reserved instances are offered at a significant discount (up to 75%) over on-demand instances. With convertible reserved instances, you can change families, operating system types, and clients while still paying the reserved instances price.

☐ **Spot instances** - Spot (spot price - the price of an exchange commodity subject to immediate payment) instances allow you to bid your price for free Amazon EC2 compute resources. Because spot instances are often available at a discount compared to on-demand pricing, they can be used to significantly reduce application execution costs, increase compute resources and application throughput without increasing your budget, and enable new types of cloud computing applications.

Amazon EC2 Container Service

Amazon EC2 Container Service (ECS) is a highly scalable, high-performance container management service that supports Docker containers (**Docker is an open source containerisation platform that can be used to automate application creation, delivery and management**). The platform allows you to test and deploy applications faster, run the required number of containers on a single machine. You can easily run applications in a managed cluster of Amazon EC2 instances. Amazon EC2 eliminates the need to install, operate, and scale your own cluster management infrastructure. With simple API requests, you can start and stop Docker container-enabled applications, query the full state of the cluster, and access many familiar features such as security groups, Elastic Load Balancing, Amazon Elastic Block Store (Amazon EBS) volumes, and AWS Identity and Access Management (IAM) roles. Using the

Amazon ECS service, you can schedule the placement of containers in your cluster based on resource needs and availability requirements. In addition, you can integrate your own or third-party scheduler into the service to meet business and application requirements.

Amazon EC2 Container Registry

Amazon EC2 Container Registry (ECR) is a fully managed Docker container registry that makes it easy for developers to store, control, and deploy Docker container images. Amazon ECR is integrated with Amazon EC2 Container Service (ECS), making it easy to get your workflow up and running. Plus, with Amazon ECR, you don't have to build your own container repositories or worry about scaling the infrastructure that powers them. Amazon ECR hosts your images in a scalable, high-availability architecture that allows you to deploy application containers reliably. With integration with AWS Identity and Access Management (IAM), you can control each repository at the resource level. You can get started with Amazon ECR service without upfront fees or any commitment. You pay only for the amount of data stored in your repositories and transmitted to the Internet.

Along with virtual machines, Amazon provides several **storage mechanisms**:

❖ *Simple Storage Service (S3) is a* storage service that provides access based on REST and SOAP. The S3 system is distributed all over the world: servers are located in Europe, Asia and the USA. It provides the ability to work with data ranging in size from a single byte to 5TB.

❖ *Elastic Block Storage (EBS) is a* high-performance virtual hard drive ranging in size from 1 GB to 1 TB. It can be attached to any virtual machine running within EC2 or placed in long-term storage on an S3 system.

❖ *Relational database services are* web services that provide installation, management and scaling of relational databases in the cloud. Currently, support for MySQL-based databases is provided (Oracle databases are planned to be introduced in the future).

❖ *Amazon CloudFront is a* web service for content delivery. Static and streaming data transfer is provided. Due to the distributed infrastructure of the system, CloudFront can ensure minimal latency of information delivery by selecting the server that is geographically closest to the user.

One of the distinctive features of the platform provided by Amazon is the provision of **application integration services** that provide transparent addressing and accessibility:

❖ *Elastic IP* provides binding of a static IP address to the user account. In this case, in case of errors and failures in the work of individual virtual machines, the IP address is automatically reassigned to another virtual machine.

❖ **Simple** Queue **Service (SQS)** provides developers with a virtually infinite number of queues. Each authorised application can register in the queue, send, receive or delete messages. Unreceived messages can remain in the system for up to 4 days.

❖ *Simple Notification Service (SNS)* is a service that provides state change notification by subscription. System users, cloud applications and devices can send and receive notifications from the cloud.

Also, Amazon is now entering the enterprise market by providing *virtual private cloud* services that extend the capabilities of corporate computing infrastructures. Essentially, it offers Virtual Private Networks (VPNs) that provide secure and transparent communications between the internal corporate network and EC2. Import of corporate virtual machines is provided, as well as the ability to transfer virtual machines on physical media, bypassing the Internet (increasing the reliability and security of data transfer).

The solution offered by Amazon Web Services provides the greatest possible flexibility in the development and deployment of cloud solutions. The most active users of this platform are large organisations, or projects that require maximum scalability and development flexibility. That said, this solution can be overly complex and burdensome for individual developers or applications that do not require such powerful scaling mechanisms.

Amazon S3

Amazon Simple Storage Service (Amazon S3) is an online web service offered by *Amazon Web Services that* provides the ability to store and retrieve any amount of data, anytime from anywhere on the network, aka file hosting. With *Amazon S3,* scalability, reliability, high speed and low-cost storage infrastructure is achieved. It first appeared in March 2006 in the US and in November 2007 in Europe.

Amazon Simple Storage Service (Amazon S3) is object storage with a simple web services interface for storing and retrieving any amount of data from virtually any resource on the network. The storage provides 99.999999999% storage reliability and scales to more than trillions of objects worldwide.

Amazon S3 can be used as primary storage for applications that were originally envisioned for the cloud; as a mass repository or "data lake" for analytics; and as a backup and recovery (including disaster recovery) target; as well as for serverless computing.

Amazon's various cloud migration capabilities make it easy to move large amounts of data in and out of Amazon S3. Once data is saved in Amazon S3, it can be automatically moved to more cost-effective cloud storage tiers for long-term storage, such as Amazon S3 Standard (rare access) and Amazon Glacier (archiving).

Amazon S3 is used by many other services to store and host files. For example, *Dropbox* and *Ubuntu One* file storage and sharing services, *Twitter* website, *Minecraft* game downloader.

Amazon S3 is a cloud storage system for the Internet.

Amazon S3 provides a simple web services interface that can be used to store and retrieve any amount of data, anytime, from anywhere on the network. It gives the developer access to the same scalable, reliable, secure, fast, low-cost infrastructure that *Amazon* uses to run its own global network of websites.

Amazon S3 features

Amazon S3 is the most feature-rich object storage cloud platform available today.

□ **Simplicity**. The Service Management Console web interface and mobile app make working with Amazon S3 simple and easy. Amazon S3 also provides full-featured REST APIs and SDKs for easy integration with third-party technologies.

□ **Reliability**. Amazon S3 resilient infrastructure provides 99.999999999% reliable storage for objects. Data backups are distributed across multiple sites and multiple devices at each site.

□ **Scalability**. Amazon S3 lets you choose how much data you want to store and how you want to access it. You no longer need to calculate the amount of resources required: scaling freely as needed helps you achieve the highest flexibility.

□ **Security**. Amazon S3 supports SSL data transfer with automatic encryption when the download is complete. In addition, you can configure cart management policies and then use them to manage object permissions and control data access using IAM.

□ **Availability**. Amazon S3 Standard delivers 99.99% availability for a given year; this service is covered by the Amazon S3 Service Level Agreement, ensuring a high level of reliability. In addition, you can select a region to optimise latency, reduce costs and ensure regulatory compliance.

□ **Low cost**. Amazon S3 is all about storing massive amounts of data at a very low cost. Using lifecycle policies, you can set up automatic migration of your data as it becomes obsolete to standard infrequent access storage or to Amazon Glacier for even greater savings.

□ **Easy data transfer**. Amazon's various cloud data migration capabilities make it easy and cost-effective to move large amounts of data to and from Amazon S3. You can choose methods to import data to and export data to and from Amazon S3 with network-optimised, physical disk-based, or third-party connectors.

□ **Integration**. Amazon S3 is deeply integrated with other AWS services, making it easy to develop end-to-end solutions using multiple AWS services at once. The service integrates with Amazon CloudFront, Amazon CloudWatch, Amazon Kinesis, Amazon RDS, Amazon Glacier, Amazon EBS, Amazon DynamoDB, Amazon Redshift, Amazon Route, Amazon EMR, Amazon VPC, Amazon Key Management Service (KMS), and AWS Lambda.

□ **Ease of management**. Amazon S3 Storage Management capabilities enable you to approach storage optimisation, data security, and management efficiency from a data-optimised perspective. These enterprise-class capabilities provide customers with data about their stored data and allow you to manage storage with customised metadata.

The future of AWS

Amazon Web Services (AWS) is a popular cloud services platform. AWS is used by many organisations and individuals around the world. AWS is worldwide and provides more than 100 services in different types. AWS supports a highly reliable, scalable and low cost cloud infrastructure platform. AWS offers many big data and application analytics services. AWS can match the era defining cloud service provider. This further increases the attention and expectations of cloud users/providers. People are willing to partner with AWS because of the centre of attraction built around it.

Amazon Web Services (AWS) Is a popular platform for cloud services. AWS has deployed several data centres around the world, especially in North America, so performance will be good compared to Azure. Amazon web service is the leading cloud service in the current market. Services offered by AWS, *Storage, Database, Migration, Networking and content delivery, Developer tools, Management tools, Media services, Machine learning, Analytics, Security, Identity and compliance, AR and VR, Application integration, Customer interaction, Business productivity, Desktop and app string, Game development.* Low cost and easy to manage global infrastructure. Future Ease of use, flexibility, cost effective, reliability, high performance, security.

The future of AWS (Amazon Web Service) is clear. Many companies like it (*Adobe, Airbnb, Alcatel-Lucent, AOL, Acquia, AdRoll, AEG, Alert Logic,*

Autodesk, Bitdefender, BMW, British Gas, Canon, Capital One, Channel 4, Chef, Citrix, Coinbase, Comcast, Coursera, Docker, Dow Jones, European Space Agency, Financial Times, FINRA, General Electric, GoSquared, Guardian News & Media, etc.) Use a cloud service

AWS in your organisation as it offers a lot of services to its customers.

Amazon Elastic Block Store

Amazon Elastic Block Store (Amazon EBS) provides persistent block-level storage volumes that can be used in the AWS cloud with Amazon EC2 instances. Each Amazon EBS volume is automatically replicated in its availability zone, providing component failure protection, high availability, and reliability. Amazon EBS volumes deliver the crash-free and latency-free performance you need to run user workloads. Amazon EBS provides the ability to scale resources in any direction in minutes, and you pay only for prepared resources at a very competitive price.

Amazon EBS capabilities

☐ **High-performance volumes**. Choose from solid state drive (SSD) or hard disk drive (HDD) based volumes to deliver the performance your most demanding applications require.

☐ **Availability**. Each Amazon EBS volume provides 99.999% design availability and automatically replicates to its availability zone, ensuring that applications are protected in the event of component failure.

☐ **Encryption**. Amazon EBS encryption effectively supports data handling during storage and transfer between EC2 instances and EBS volumes.

☐ **Access Control**. Amazon's flexible access control policies allow you to determine who is allowed to access EBS volumes. This approach ensures secure access to your data.

☐ **State Snapshots**. State snapshots of EBS volumes at a point in time are used to protect data and are sent to Amazon S3 for long-term storage.

Amazon Elastic File System

Amazon Elastic File System (Amazon EFS) is a simple, scalable file storage designed for use with Amazon EC2 instances in the AWS cloud. Amazon EFS is easy to use with a user-friendly interface that makes it quick and easy to create and configure file systems. With Amazon EFS, storage capacity becomes elastic, meaning it increases or decreases automatically as files are added and deleted. Now your applications will always have the storage capacity they need.

The Amazon EFS file system, when connected to Amazon EC2 instances, provides a standard interface and semantics for file system access, allowing you to efficiently integrate Amazon EFS with existing applications and tools.

Multiple EC2 instances can simultaneously access the EFS file system. In this way, Amazon EFS serves as a common data source for workloads and applications running across multiple Amazon EC2 instances.

You can host your Amazon EFS file systems on servers in your local data centre by connecting to the VPC cloud using AWS Direct Connect. You can host your Amazon EFS file systems on local servers to migrate datasets to EFS, enable rapid cloud scaling, or back up local data to EFS.

Amazon EFS is designed to meet the most stringent requirements for high availability and storage reliability. Its performance makes the service suitable for a very wide range of workloads and applications, including big data and analytics, media workflows, content management, website maintenance, and home directories.

Amazon Glacier

Amazon Glacier is a secure, reliable and extremely cost-effective storage service for archiving and long-term data backup storage. You can securely store large and small amounts of data for as low as 0.004 USD per gigabyte per month, which is much more cost-effective than on-premises solutions. To keep costs low and meet different data retrieval needs, Amazon Glacier offers three archive access options, ranging from a few minutes to a few hours.

AWS Storage Gateway

AWS Storage Gateway service makes it easy to organise hybrid storage using local storage and the AWS cloud. It combines multi-protocol storage devices and high-performance network connectivity to Amazon cloud storage services to deliver performance levels comparable to on-premises storage with virtually unlimited scalability. This service can be used in remote offices and data centres for hybrid cloud workloads, including data migration, rapid cloud scaling, and tiered storage.

Database

Amazon Aurora

Amazon Aurora is a MySQL- and PostgreSQL-compatible relational database engine that combines the speed and availability of expensive commercial databases with the simplicity and cost-effectiveness of open source databases. Amazon Aurora's performance is five times faster than MySQL; it provides the security, availability, and reliability of a commercial database; and it costs ten times less.

Advantages

□ **High performance**. Amazon Aurora delivers up to five times the throughput of a standard MySQL database running on the same hardware and twice the throughput of a standard PostgreSQL database. You get consistently high performance of commercial databases at a price ten times lower than its peers. On the largest Amazon Aurora instance, you can achieve about 500,000 reads and 100,000 writes per second. It is possible to further scale read operations using read replicas with very low latency, just over 10 milliseconds.

High level of security. Amazon Aurora provides several layers of database security. These include network isolation using Amazon VPC, encryption of data at rest using keys you create and control in AWS Key Management Service (KMS), and encryption of data in transit using SSL. An encrypted Amazon Aurora instance encrypts the underlying storage data, as well as automatically created backups, state snapshots, and replicas that reside in the same cluster.

□ **MySQL and PostgreSQL support**. The Amazon Aurora database core is fully compatible with MySQL 5.6 when using the InnoDB storage core. This means that much of the code, applications, drivers, and tools that already work with MySQL databases can be used with Amazon Aurora with little or no modification. It also makes it easy to migrate existing MySQL databases using standard MySQL import and export tools or MySQL binary log replication. A preview version of PostgreSQL-compatible Amazon Aurora database instances is currently available, which supports the SQL dialect and functionality of PostgreSQL 9.6.

□ **High Scalability**. The Amazon Aurora database scales from an instance with 2 virtual CPUs and 4 GB of memory to an instance with 32 virtual CPUs and 244 GB of memory. You can also add up to 15 low-latency read replicas across three availability zones to further scale the amount of read resources. Amazon Aurora automatically grows storage from 10 GB to 64 TB as needed.

□ **High availability and reliability**. Amazon Aurora provides higher than 99.99% availability. Recovery from physical storage failures is seamless to the user, and instance failure handling typically takes less than 30 seconds. Amazon Aurora storage is fault-tolerant and self-healing. Six copies of your data are replicated across three availability zones, with regular backups and subsequent storage in Amazon S3.

□ **Fully Managed**. Amazon Aurora is a fully managed database service. You no longer need to deal with database administration tasks such as allocating necessary hardware, installing software patches, setup, configuration, monitoring and backups. Amazon Aurora automatically and continuously monitors the database and backs up to S3, ensuring accurate recovery at a given point in time.

Google Platform Overview

Examples of Google cloud services

Brief lecture abstract:

This lecture discusses several cloud services provided by Google.

Purpose of the lecture:

Familiarise yourself with the main cloud service solutions. Understand the principles of providing and using cloud services.

Google Apps

Google Apps is an environment that provides the following collaboration tools: the already popular mail service GMail, instant messaging client Google Talk (in fact, the service is fully suitable for communication with any jabber-user), Google Calendar, tools for working with documents and spreadsheets Google Docs & Spreadsheets, "central page" - a place for convenient placement of information that will be common for all users, page editor from Google, which allows you to quickly create and publish the desired information.

Functions available to the user

Describing all the features that are available to every user of the Google Apps system is quite a long task, as the system combines several rather flexible products from Google, each of which has already successfully proven itself. In addition, most of these services are quite popular individually.

To begin with, Google Apps is a serious service that has several packages, each of which is characterised by a different number of services provided by Google. All packages provide: a full set of services (mail, calendar, work with documents, page creation, quick messaging client and so on), no restrictions on the number of user accounts, access from mobile devices, administrator control panel. Thus, the basic set, which is provided to all users, is approximately the same, in addition, there is a system of migration from one package to another, which allows you to start with a simpler and free package, and later, if necessary, migrate to a suitable package with the necessary additions. The main differences are as follows.

The best place to start is with the standard Google Apps package. It's free

• Standard Edition - 2 gigabytes of free space for mail, help via online resources (but not online telephone help), presence of contextual advertising on the pages of services.

• Premier Edition - 10 gigabytes of mail, 99.9% guaranteed *uptime for* mail, resource management capabilities, 24/7 online help that includes phone consultations, APIs to best integrate Google Apps into your existing infrastructure. The only one of all packages that is not free. The cost of this package depends on the number of user accounts. Users of the package get access to all new features and services as they are released, for example, in the near future the service of migration from other email clients, which will allow migration with the least effort.

• Education Edition - everything is the same as in the previous case. The only difference: only 2 gigabytes per account, no 99.9% uptime guarantee. The package is available under a separate licence for non-commercial educational organisations.

Once the administrator who works with Google Apps has added a user to the system (Google Apps domain), the user can work with all the services that are included in the system. One of the main ideas of Google Apps is global integration of all services and organisation of convenient work of people who are united by a common Google Apps system. This saves a lot of time in organising collaboration, as the work environment is ready for use in just a few minutes after full activation.

Mail and messaging

Once the mail service related to the domain is activated, it will be available to users on a special page, the name of which is determined by the system administrator. If the domain settings allow it, all domain users will be automatically added to the contacts of each new system user.

Frequently Mailed   All Contacts   Groups   Search Contacts

Name   Details

Alexel 'keyhel   keyhell@keyhell.org

User Test   test_user@keyhell.org

Fig. 12.1 Contact list

All domain users are automatically present in the address book

Similarly with the Quick Messaging client: new domain users will be automatically added to the client's contact list. This provides an instant start of the user's work after he/she is registered in the system. It is no longer necessary to add each colleague to the contact list separately.

Obviously, users get all the standard features of Google mail service: mail archiving, spam filtering, the ability to search through all mail messages, creating filters, POP access, mail forwarding and much more. The same can be said about Google Talk - all functions are available in full, and the administrator can limit the ability of users to add users from other domains or from other jabber-servers to the contact list, which allows you to limit the circle of communication only to the necessary contacts.

Calendar

A very convenient tool for planning personal working time, which in the context of global integration allows you to plan not only your own working time, but also to take into account the working time and tasks of your colleagues. The main features of the calendar in Google Apps: creating events, for each of which you can define the name of the event, time and duration, defining the composition of participants and checking their employment during the event, setting reminders about events, viewing other people's calendars, working with the calendar on mobile devices, managing access to calendars, and so on.

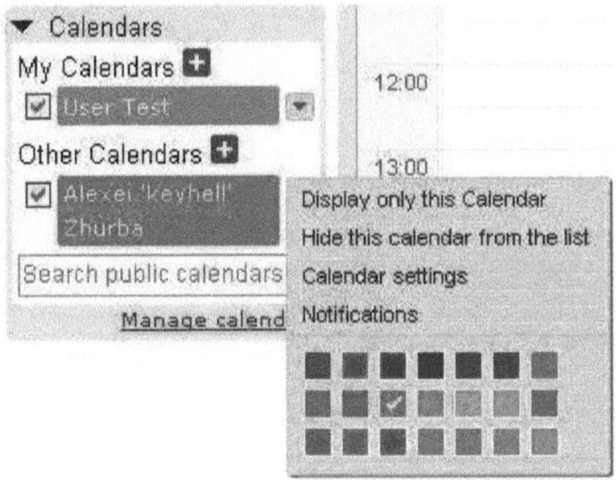

Fig. 12.2. Viewing events in another user's calendar

A domain user can add a particular employee's calendar using a special form that allows searching calendars using both keywords and the employee's e-mail address. In this way, it is possible to always have up-to-date information about tasks and work of a certain employee (obviously, only to the extent that his/her calendar can be identified).

Document handling

All popular document formats are supported: Word, Excel, OpenOffice

Currently, it is possible to work with the following file types: Word and Excel documents, OpenOffice documents, RTF, HTML and text documents. This set of supported formats ensures that the service is suitable for a wide range of users. The results of work can be saved either to a local computer or left for storage on the server. Thus, for full-fledged work with documents it is enough just to have access to the Google Apps service from anywhere in the world, from any computer.

Comparing the features of Google Docs & *Spreadsheets* editors themselves with Word and Excel or OpenOffice is a topic for a separate discussion. Practical use shows that the functions are enough to prepare a normal document that contains commonly used design elements: lists, formatting and various styles, tables, images and hyperlinks, and so on.

Google Docs & *Spreadsheets* provides a wide range of ways to collaborate on documents. To make document collaboration as convenient and productive as possible for a group of employees, the following options are available.

• Document version management. Intermediate versions of the document are created by the system automatically quite often and, in addition, every time the user saves the document. The function of comparing two selected versions is available, which makes it easy to keep track of the changes that have been made by the next document editing.

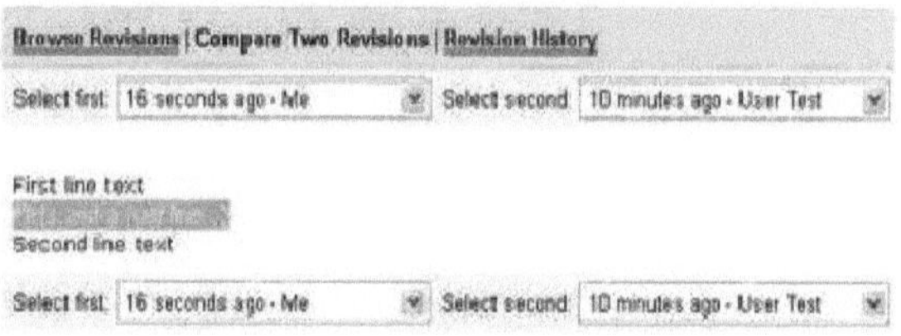

Fig. 12.3. Version comparison

Changes between versions of the document are highlighted in green colour

• Document access control. You can invite users of the system to work with a document, specifying what rights are given to the user: only to view the document or to edit it. Additional features allow a user invited to work with a document to invite other users in turn. People who work with the document at the same time can have a chat to discuss changes in the document, which will be visible to all participants of the discussion. It is possible to publish a document with a permanent address, which allows any employee of the domain to access the document (for example, after all changes are made and approved, the document is published for public review). In addition, it is possible to archive documents that have already been brought to their final state but may still be needed.

Document collaboration in Google Apps is organised at a high level, sufficient for working with documents and accessing shared information quickly and efficiently. And user functions for editing document content are only in some aspects inferior to the familiar Word, Excel and OpenOffice.

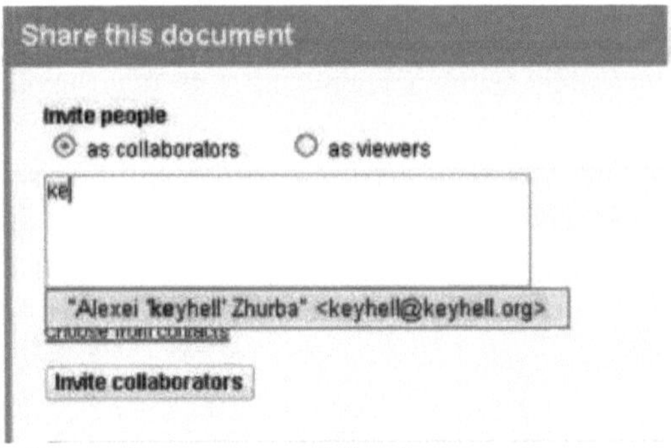

Fig. 12.4. Invitation to the user to read the document

Start page and page editor

The start page is the first thing users will see after logging into Google Apps. *The Start page is* the place that is designed to be the first thing users see after logging in to Google Apps. This page is similar to Google's personal page (*www.www.igoogle.com.com*), in the same way that it is designed to be the first page a user encounters when starting out. It can host gadgets from Google and third-party developers, as well as information that employees need to get started. The list of useful things that can be placed on the Google Apps start page is far from complete: gadgets for previewing personal mailboxes and calendar events, search, including Google Custom Search, which allows you to search only what you really need, RSS, bookmarks, Google *Notebook* and many more useful elements.

Google App Engine

Google App Engine lets you run your web applications on Google's infrastructure. *App Engine* applications are easy to create, maintain, and enhance as traffic and storage increases. With *App Engine,* you don't need to maintain a *server*: just upload your *application* and users can work with it.

The application can be published in its own domain (e.g, *http://http://www.example.com.example.com*) using Google services. Or use the free domain name appspot. *com.* You can make the app available to everyone or give *access* only to members of your team.

Google *App Engine* supports applications written in multiple programming languages. With the *Java App Engine* runtime environment, you can create applications using standard *Java* technologies, including the *JVM, Java servlets,* and the *Java* programming language, or another language that uses an *interpreter* or *compiler* on the *JVM,* such as JavaScript or *Ruby. In* addition, *App Engine* provides a dedicated *Python* runtime environment that includes a fast *interpreter* and a standard *Python* library. The *Java* and

Python runtime environments are specifically designed to allow applications to run quickly and safely without interacting with other applications on the system.

You only have to pay for what you use, Google *App Engine*. There are no installation fees or recurring charges. You *pay* for resources used by the app, such as storage and traffic measured in gigabytes, at reasonable rates. You can manage the maximum amount of resources the *app* can use, allowing you to always stay within budget.

It's free to start using *App Engine*. You do not have to pay for apps that use less than 500MB of storage, nor do you have to pay for CPU resources and traffic sufficient for an efficient app serving up to five million page views per month. By enabling payment for an app, these limits are raised, and you're only charged for resources used beyond the free tiers.

The user accesses the cloud application through a web browser. Google App Engine currently supports development based on Python and all languages that can be executed inside the Java Virtual Machine (Java, Jython, Scala, etc.). Google App Engine developers are provided with a development kit (SDK) that includes a full-fledged simulation of Google App Engine running on a working machine.

Google App Engine provides a large **set of library functions to perform standard operations**:

❖ of working with mail messages;
❖ user authorisation and authentication;
❖ image processing;
❖ loading and processing web pages;
❖ task planning;
❖ data processing through **MapReduce** (a distributed computing model used for parallel computing over very large, several petabytes, data sets in computer clusters);
❖ storing large (up to 2 GB) amounts of information;
❖ messaging based on **XMPP (Jabber)** (**Extensible Messaging and Presence Protocol** - an XML-based, open, free-to-use protocol for instant messaging and near real-time presence information exchange).

Google App Engine enables the ability to deliver a high-performance service without significant infrastructure costs.

Figure 12.5: Running Google App Engine in the cloud

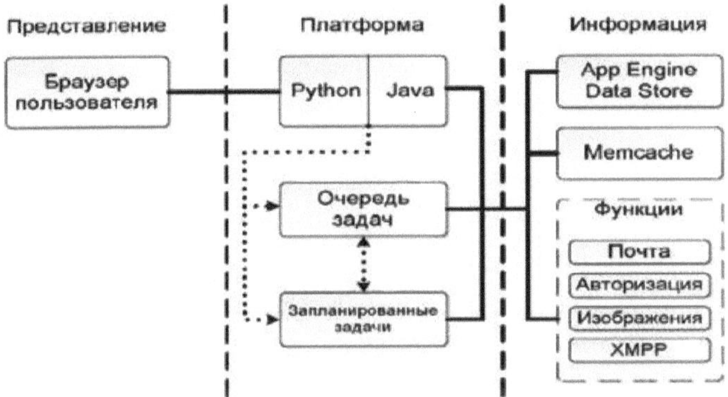

Figure 12.6: Google App Engine architecture

App Engine Datastore is a highly distributed data storage system based on the proprietary BigTable database developed by Google. The methods of working with the store are very different from those of relational databases. The main difference is that there are no data schemas in App Engine Datastore. All data is stored in the form of blocks "key"-"value"-"timestamp". Accordingly, all responsibility for the compliance of the stored data with the business logic of the application falls on the developer.

Special libraries are provided in the SDK to ensure data consistency. Google has developed its own query language (GQL), similar to SELECT statements in SQL, but with more restrictions.

The need to **work within a "sandbox"** (a virtual machine with limited access to local resources). For example, the set of protocols and ports through which the application can communicate with the outside world is significantly restricted (practically the possibility of communication only through HTTP and HTTPS is left). Also, the application is not allowed to work with the local file system (only reading files that were downloaded together with the application code is allowed).

Application environment

Google *App Engine* makes it easy to create applications that work reliably even under heavy load and with large amounts of data. *App Engine* includes the following features:

- dynamic web experience with full support for major web technologies;
- persistent storage with queries, sorting, and transactions;
- automatic scaling and load regulation;
- API to authenticate users and send emails using Google accounts;
- A full-featured local development environment that mimics Google App Engine on your computer;
- scheduled tasks to track events at specific times or at regular intervals.

An application can run in one of two runtime environments: *Java* and *Python.* Each environment provides standard protocols and core technologies for web application development.

Applications run in a secure environment that provides limited *access to* the attached operating system. The restrictions allow *App Engine* to distribute web requests for the application to multiple servers, and to start and stop servers based on traffic. The test environment isolates your *application* in its own secure and reliable environment, independent of the hardware, operating system, and physical location of the web server.

The following are examples of the limitations of a robust test environment.

The application can *access* other computers on the Internet only through the provided *APIs, URL retrieval service* and email service. Other computers can only connect to the application by *HTTP requests* (or HTTPS requests) on standard ports.

The application cannot *write* to the file system. The *application* can read files, but only those that were downloaded with the application code. The *application* must use the *App Engine data store,* memory *cache,* and other services for all data stored between requests.

Application code is executed only in response to a *web* request or Cron task and must return response data within 30 seconds in either case. The request handler cannot create a *subprocess* or execute code after the response has been sent.

An application can be developed for the *Java* runtime environment using standard *Java* web development tools and standard *APIs. The application* interacts with the environment using the *Java Servlet* standard and can use standard web application technologies such as JavaServer Pages (*JSP*).

The Java runtime environment uses *Java 6. The Java App Engine SDK* supports application development using *Java 5* and 6.

The environment includes the *Java* SE Runtime *Environment (JRE)* 6 platform and libraries. The test environment constraints are implemented in the *JVM. An application* can use byte code from the *JVM* or libraries within the constraints of the test environment. For example, if byte code attempts to open a *socket* or write a *file, a* runtime environment *exception* will occur.

Most *App Engine* services can be *accessed* through standard *Java APIs.* For the *App Engine* data store, the *Java SDK* contains implementations of the *Java* Data Object *(JDO)* and *Java Persistence API* (JPA) interfaces. To send email messages using the *Mail App Engine* service, *you* can use the JavaMail *API*. The *HTTP java API. net* has *access* to the *App Engine's URL* retrieval service. *In* addition, for its services, *App Engine* includes low-level *APIs* that implement additional adapters and allow you to use the services directly from within the application. Check out the documentation for *APIs for* data store, memory cache, *URL fetch,* mail, images, and Google accounts.

Typically, *Java* developers use the *Java programming language* and *APIs* to develop web applications for the *JVM.* Using JVM-compatible compilers and interpreters, it is possible to develop web applications in other languages such as JavaScript, *Ruby,* and Scala.

With the *Python App Engine* runtime environment, you can create applications using the *Python* programming language and run them using an optimised *Python* interpreter. *App Engine* includes a variety of *APIs* and tools for developing *Python* web applications, including an enriched data modelling *API,* an easy-to-use web application framework, and tools for managing and accessing application data. You can take advantage of a wide range of libraries and frameworks, such as Django, to develop *Python* web applications.

The Python runtime environment uses *Python* version 2.5.2. Support for *Python 3 is* being considered for a future release.

The Python environment contains the standard *Python* library. Naturally, not all library functions can be used in the test environment. For example, calling a method that opens a *socket* or writes to a *file will* raise an *exception.* For convenience, several modules of the standard library, whose key functions are not supported by the runtime environment, are disabled. Executing code importing them will cause an error.

Application code created for the *Python* environment must be written exclusively in *Python*. Extensions written in C are not supported.

The Python environment provides powerful *Python APIs* for data storage services, Google accounts, *URL* retrieval, and email. *App Engine* also provides a simple *Python* web application framework called webapp that makes it easy to create applications.

Third-party libraries can be loaded with the application, but they must be implemented in pure *Python* and must not require unsupported standard library modules.

App Engine provides a powerful distributed data storage service that includes a query engine and transactions. Extending a distributed *database with* data is similar to extending a distributed web server with traffic.

The App Engine data store is not like a normal relational database. Data objects, or "records", have a view and a set of properties. Queries can retrieve records of a particular view, filtered and sorted by property values. Property values can be any of the supported property value types.

A schema is not required for data warehouse objects. The structure of data objects is defined in the application code. The *Java* JDO/JPA and *Python data warehouse* interfaces include functions to apply the structure to the application. The *application* can *directly access the data* store to implement the desired part of the structure.

The data warehouse is consistent and uses optimistic concurrent transaction management. A record is updated in a transaction that is executed repeatedly a certain number of times if other processes concurrently attempt to update the same *record. An application* can perform multiple operations on a data store in a single transaction. These *operations* will either all succeed or all fail, ensuring *data integrity*.

A data warehouse implements transactions in its distributed network using "record groups". A *transaction* performs actions on records in one group. The records in each group are stored together for efficient transaction execution. When records are created, the *application* can attach them to groups.

App Engine supports application integration with Google accounts for user authentication. Your *app* can allow a user to sign in to their Google account and *access the* email address and display name associated with the account. Using Google accounts gives the user a quicker way to start using your *app* because they don't have to create a new account. It also removes the need for you to implement a user account system just for your app.

If the *app* is running on Google Services, it can use the same features for your organisation's members and Google Services accounts.

The user *API* can also tell the application whether the current *user* is a registered administrator of the application. This simplifies the implementation of administrative areas of the site.

The App Engine provides a set of services that allow you to perform common operations when managing an application. The following *APIs are* provided to access these services.

Applications can *access* resources on the Internet, such as web services or other data, using *App Engine's URL retrieval service*. The *URL retrieval* service retrieves web resources through the same high-speed Google infrastructure that retrieves web pages for many other Google products.

- **Email**

Applications can send email messages using the App Engine email service. This service uses Google's infrastructure to send emails.

- **Memcache**

The Memcache service provides your application with a high-performance memory cache using a key-value structure that can be accessed by multiple instances of the application. The memory cache comes in handy for data that does not require persistent storage and the transactional functionality that the data store provides, such as temporary data or data that is copied from the store to the cache to speed up access.

- **Working with images**

The Image Service allows the application to work with images. You can use this API to resize, crop, rotate, and reflect JPEG and PNG images.

- **Scheduled tasks**

The Cron service allows you to schedule tasks to run at specific intervals. You can learn more about it in the Python and Java Cron service documentation.

- **Development process**

The App Engine Development Kit (SDK) for Java and Python includes a web server application that mimics App Engine services on a local computer. Each SDK includes all the APIs and libraries available in App Engine. In addition, the web server simulates a secure test environment that includes system resource access checks that are not allowed in App Engine.

Each SDK also includes a tool for adding an application to the App Engine. After creating the app code, static files, and configuration files, run this tool to upload the data. The tool will ask for your Google account email address and password.

When you create a new release of an app that is already running in App Engine, you will be able to upload it as a new version. The old version will work for users until you upgrade to the new version. You can test the new version in App Engine while the old version is running.

The Java SDK runs on any platform with Java 5 or Java 6. The SDK is available as a ZIP file. When using the Eclipse development environment, you can use the Google plugin for Eclipse to create, test, and add App Engine applications. The SDK also contains command-line tools to run the development server and add applications.

The Python SDK is implemented in pure Python and runs on any platform with Python 2.5, including Windows, Mac OS X and Linux. The SDK is available as a Zip file, and installers are available for Windows and Mac OS X.

The Administration Console is a web-based interface for managing applications running in the App Engine. You can use it to create new applications, configure domain names, change the working version of an application, examine access and error logs, and view the application's data store.

- **Quotas and restrictions**

Creating an app in App Engine is not only easy, it's free! You can create an account and publish an app that can be used immediately, for free and with no additional requirements. An app with a free account can use up to 500MB of data storage and up to five million page views per month. If you need more, enable payment, set a maximum daily budget and distribute it among resources according to your needs.

Up to 10 apps can be registered for a developer account.

Each application is allocated resources within limits or "quotas". A quota defines the amount of a particular resource that can be used in a calendar day. It will soon be possible to customise some of these quotas by paying for additional resources.

For some functions, the limits are not related to quotas, but are intended to preserve system stability. For example, if an application is called to make a web request, it must create a response within 30 seconds. If this process takes too long, it is terminated and the server returns an error code to the user. The request timeout is dynamic and can be decreased to conserve resources if the request handler reaches it too often.

Another example of a service limitation is the number of results returned by a query. A query can return no more than 1000 results. Queries that could return more will only return the maximum number allowed. In this case, such a query most likely will not return results before the timeout occurs, but thanks to the limitation, data storage resources will be saved.

Attempts to bypass or exceed quotas, such as by running applications in multiple shared accounts, violate the Terms of Service and may result in the disabling of applications or termination of accounts.

For a list of quotas and an explanation of the quota system, including quotas that can be increased by including payment, see the article Quotas.

Summary of results:

In this lecture, we have looked at some of the most prominent examples of cloud services. The number of these services is constantly increasing. More and more ideas and startups are being implemented in the cloud. All this testifies to the popularity of these technologies.

Windows Azure **Platform Overview**

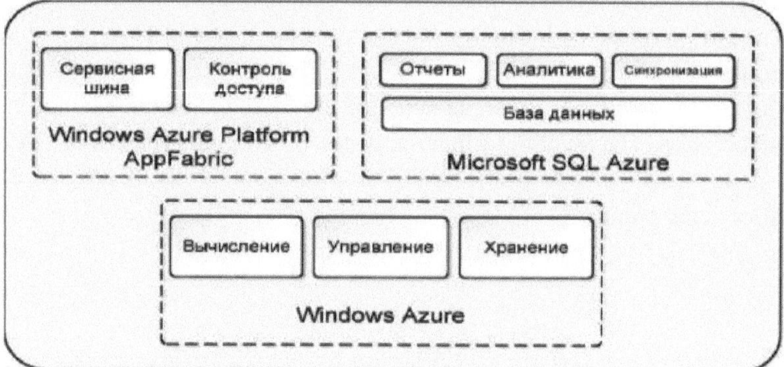

Figure 13.1: Architecture of Microsoft Windows Azure

Windows Azure platform allows to run applications developed on the basis of Microsoft.NET platform on Microsoft servers, providing automatic management of computing resources, load balancing and data replication. Developer access to the platform is provided by means of tools integrated into the latest versions of Visual Studio (Windows Azure SDK, Windows Azure Tools for MVS). At the same time, local testing of applications before their publication on the Azure service is supported.

The Windows Azure platform consists of **three main components**:

* computational entities;
* storage entities;
* factories.

Computational entities are containers for applications that support modern development technologies including .NET, Java, PHP, Python, Ruby on Rails, and native code.

Computing entities can fulfil **2 main roles**:

* *A Web Role* is a web application available to a user over the internet that can be accessed through a web browser.

* *A Worker Role* is an application that performs some computational load in the background (something like a service in Microsoft Windows).

Storage entities are a set of services that provide data storage.

Each service provides a different type of data storage.

* *Binary objects* - provides storage of large sets of unstructured bytes (files). It is possible to name files and work with metadata. The maximum size of the stored file is not more than 1 TB.

❖ *Tables* - used to store structured data. Tables are a set of homogeneous rows (called entities) whose structure is defined by a set of columns (called properties). A single entity can have up to 256 properties. Tables are distributed in such a way as to maintain load balancing as much as possible

❖ *Queues* *are* *a* mechanism providing asynchronous interaction of applications by storing and transmitting messages. An unlimited number of queues can be used, and queues can contain an unlimited number of messages.

❖ *Disks* - Similar to AWS, Windows Azure allows you to manage disks within your virtual machines. Azure allows you to work with NTFS volumes, making them available to applications. This can allow for easier migration of conventional applications to the cloud, as it becomes possible to save state in the file system.

Windows Azure is an open and flexible cloud platform that enables you to quickly build, deploy and manage applications across a global network from *Microsoft-managed* datacenters. You can build applications using any language, tool or platform, and integrate public cloud applications with your existing IT environment.

High Availability. *Windows Azure* offers a 99.95 per cent monthly service level agreement, allowing you to build and run highly available applications without focusing on infrastructure. This platform has the ability to automatically apply OS and service patches, built-in network load balancing and resilience to hardware failures. It supports a deployment model that allows you to update your application with zero downtime.

Openness. *Windows Azure* allows you to use any language, any tool, or any platform to build applications. Components and services are provided using open *REST* protocols. *Windows Azure* client libraries are available for several programming languages, released under an open source licence and hosted on *GitHub*.

Unlimited server resources. Unlimited storage. *Windows Azure* makes it easy to scale applications to any size. It is a fully automated platform Self-service, which allows you to prepare resources for work in minutes. Flexibly expand or reduce resource utilisation according to your needs. Pay only for the resources used by your application. The *Windows Azure* platform is available in multiple data centres around the world, allowing you to deploy applications closer to your customers. Today, there are six data centres, two per region (North America, Europe, Asia).

Advanced features. The *Windows Azure* platform is a flexible cloud platform that can meet any application need. It provides reliable code placement and scalability across application execution roles. You can use *SQL* relational databases, *NoSQL* table stores, unstructured large binary object stores to store data, and if needed, use *Hadoop* components and business analytics services for data mining. The secure messaging capabilities of the *Windows Azure* platform enable the deployment of distributed applications and hybrid solutions that run in a mixed cloud and on-premises enterprise environment. By leveraging distributed caching or a caching server network (*CDN*), you can reduce latency and improve application timing across the globe. The *Windows Azure* platform provides a set of services that are largely similar to those used by developers of "traditional" applications.

Compute Services. These are containers for applications with support for modern development technologies, including *.NET, Java, PHP, Python, Ruby on Rails* and native code.

Storage Services. A scalable distributed storage system that supports a range of storage models, including table structures, binary objects, asynchronous message queues, traditional file systems and *CDNs* (*content distribution networks*).

Communication Services. Available via the cloud service bus and can be used as a messaging tool or connection broker to other cloud or customer-hosted services.

Security services. Policy-based access control services that support federation mechanisms and allow integration with existing identity management systems.

Application Services. Components and services that can be used to develop cloud applications and application services.

Cloud platform components

The Windows Azure platform consists of the following major components:
- *web sites*;
- virtual machines;
- mobile services;
- cloud services;
- large volumes of data (storage);
- multimedia.

For each component, different usage scenarios are possible, and they may include multiple components.

Web sites

Web development is one of the fastest growing trends. The evolution of the Internet and the technologies that provide access to it requires new tools and models for deploying sites and ensuring their high availability and reliability. Traditional hosting services remain popular and are constantly being updated, while providing the latest versions of tools to maintain websites.

Cloud platforms allow for enhanced development capabilities and offer a high degree of scalability. They provide qualitatively new services that are characterised by greater flexibility, manageability and others. This in turn allows you to manage your costs and pay only for the resources actually needed and used, reducing costs. At first, you can start with a small site with default settings. Then, if necessary, you can select a suitable virtual machine for a highly loaded site, increase traffic, add other services such as caching, *CDN*, *SQL* databases, storage and others.

You can use open source languages and applications to create sites as you see fit, and then deploy using *FTP, Git*, and *TFS*. Using *Git* and *TFS* gives you the ability to set up automatic publishing of a site once its latest version is updated in a version control system (VCS). Setting up continuous integration and deployment removes the need for manual build, testing and deployment. All of this will be done automatically.

There are two paths you can take to create a *web site:*
-    choose a website template (from those presented in the gallery);
-    create your site (*Quick Create* or *Create With Database*).

There are many types of websites and platforms available in the gallery, such as *WordPress, KentikoCMS, Orchard CMS*, etc. In many cases, selecting applications from the existing ones will ensure faster creation of the required portal, as well as provide management capabilities.

If you create the site yourself in the control panel, you need to prepare a virtual machine for it, create a database (if necessary) and allocate storage space. In this scenario, an instance of the virtual machine on which the site will be deployed will be provided. Next, you need to choose a deployment or publishing method. Among the options are not only *Git* and *TFS*, but also *Web Deploy* and *FTP Deploy*, available in the *IDE* after selecting the publishing settings, which can be downloaded from the portal.

Once the site files have been uploaded, it can be accessed at the address that is given automatically in the third-level domain (*<your_name>.azurewebsites.net*) and has the name of your site (which was set when you created it).

If necessary, *DNS* name can be changed to your own (this is available for modes other than *Free*, and also requires a fixed fee). If it is necessary to improve site performance, increase database size, it is necessary to choose a more powerful virtual machine and database.

Virtual machines

In *Windows Azure,* you can easily use your own *Windows Server* or *Linux images*, or select images from the collection. This allows you to retain full control over the images and keep them aligned with business requirements. *Windows Azure* also helps you migrate applications and infrastructure without changing existing code, which speeds up the migration of *SharePoint, SQL Server and Active Directory* to the cloud and saves time and money.

Virtual machines should be used to gain flexibility, run applications in the cloud, and manage them remotely.

Gain flexibility. Virtual machines give your application mobility by allowing you to move virtual hard disks (*VHDs*) between on-premises and cloud environments.

Running applications in the cloud. If your company uses popular *Microsoft* server applications, virtual machines can help you run the same on-premises enterprise applications and infrastructure in the cloud. Easily work with applications such as *Microsoft SQL Server, Active Directory*, and *Microsoft SharePoint Server*.

Remote management. With full administrative access, you can remotely connect to virtual machines and manage the applications installed on them. All virtual machines are managed by *HyperV* and hosted in global data centres. Each virtual machine can have different characteristics - number of processors, amount of memory, amount of storage (hard disc).

Cloud services

Provide the ability to create applications and *APIs* with high availability and infinite scalability.

Windows Azure cloud services allow you to build applications that remain available even during software upgrades and hardware failures.

The service level agreement guarantees an availability rate of 99.95% for the application.

Every new cloud application requires a powerful set of server services. *Windows Azure* Cloud Services provides everything you need to build the most robust and scalable *APIs*.

Windows Azure cloud services provide the most efficient environment for building the most advanced distributed computing applications on the planet.

Mobile services

Windows Azure Mobile Services is a set of services designed to make it easier for mobile app developers to create and use a server backend. Using the *WindowsAzure* cloud as such a backend will provide ready-made functionality for *push notifications*, saving data to cloud storage, user authentication and authorisation without the need to deploy your own infrastructure.

Access to the services is available from *C#* and *JavaScript*. The development team is working on a public *REST API*, which will allow receiving data and working with services from any language. As of today there is official tool support for *Windows Phone, iOS, Windows* 10. *Android support is* also planned to be added.

Today, *Windows Azure Mobile Services* offers the following functionality:

- storing user data in the cloud;
- authentication and authorisation of users in the cloud;
- receiving *push notifications* from the cloud service.

Features:

- *REST API*, access from any mobile client;
- scaling on demand;
- monitoring of resource consumption and number of requests in real time;
- relational storage, support for *SQL* queries, indexes;
- automatic updating of the data schema;
- permissions, processing requests before *CRUD* operations;
- functional single control panel;
- 10 copies are available free of charge.

The latest update to the service has provided the following features:

Support for the *iOS* platform and release of a separate *iOS SDK*. Added new tools for developing *iOS* applications for *iPhone* and *iPad*. These tools are released open source under the free *Apache* 2.0 licence.

The new *SDK makes it* easier for *iOS* app developers to access information storage and authorisation services via third-party services and *Microsoft Account service*. Support for *push* notifications is not yet available in the new *iOS SDK* and will be available in the near future.

Support for third-party authorisation services: *Facebook, Twitter, Google. In* addition to the already offered *Microsoft Account* authorisation service, which you could use for your applications earlier, the update introduces support for third-party authorisation services: *Facebook, Twitter* and *Google*.

Using *Windows Azure Tables, Blobs*, and *Service Bus* inside *Mobile services*. With the service update, developers now have the ability to use calls to other cloud platform services within *Mobile Services* scripts: *Tables* and *Blobs* storage and *Service Bus* integration.

Sending mail and *SMS* messages. In addition to using the cloud services of the platform itself from the *Mobile Services* server scripts, the update adds functionality that allows you to send mail messages (using *SendGrid*) and *SMS* messages. You can send up to 25000 mail messages per month for free. Similar to sending email messages, the update introduces the ability to send *SMS* notifications. For this purpose, the *Twilio* service is used, which offers *Windows Azure* developers 1000 free messages.

High-volume data

Windows Azure provides many services to help you manage data in the cloud, called *Windows Azure Storage*. Each service is suitable for storing a specific type of data.

Tables - represent a structured storage. Each table consists of a set of objects, each of which has a set of property names and their values. One object can have up to 256 properties. Tables are distributed in such a way as to maintain load balancing as much as possible.

Binary Objects - used to store large binary objects (files). It provides a simple interface for storing named files along with metadata and supports a content distribution network. Binary objects are arranged in containers, each of which contains a set of objects.

Binary objects can be of two types - block binary objects optimised for streaming data exchange and page binary objects optimised for random I/O operations. The size of a block binary object cannot exceed 200 GB, and the size of a page binary object cannot exceed 1 TB.

***BLOB* objects are the** simplest way to store large amounts of unstructured text or binary data such as videos, music files and images. *BLOB* objects are an *ISO* 27001 certified managed service that can automatically scale to 100TB and can be accessed from virtually anywhere using *REST and* managed *APIs*.

Queues are a secure repository of messages. It is usually used to provide communication between roles. This service operates on queues that contain messages. An unlimited number of queues can be used, and queues can contain an unlimited number of messages. The size of a message is limited to 8 Kb.

Drives are *NTFS* volumes that are accessible to applications running in the *Windows Azure* infrastructure. Drives (*Windows AzureDrives*) are stored as *NTFS* formatted *Virtual Hard Drives* (*VHDs*) in paged binary objects. Because the drives support persistence, they can be used by applications that need to save states.24When a *Windows Azure drive is* mounted, it is accessible programmatically through standard *NTFS* interfaces. Using *Windows Azure disks* can greatly simplify the migration of existing applications to the *Windows Azure* platform.

Let's look at a few examples to illustrate some storage service usage scenarios.

Storage of binary objects. Possibility to store backups, reports and other things for their quick retrieval in case of need.

Tabular storage. Possibility to store web-application states, e.g. in case of e-commerce - storage of shopping basket or current order state.

Queues. A *Web* application can invoke services hosted on the *Windows Azure* platform and communicate between *Web* roles and application roles within one or more applications.

Disks. By supporting the *NTFS* file system, can be used by services to provide support for traditional read/write file operations, such as logging operations or storing temporary data.

To store relational data, for example, when moving a local database to the cloud, you should use the *Windows Azure* platform component - *SQL Azure.*

SQL Azure is a way to provide *Microsoft* relational database as a service. This server is based on *Microsoft SQL Server* technologies and provides an error-resistant, scalable, and multitenant database available as a service. As with *Windows Azure, SQL Azure* is not just about hosting *Microsoft SQL Server.*

SQL Azure's operation is based on the *Cloud Fabric* component, which manages database instances and ensures that they are deployed, administered, updated, monitored, and support the entire data lifecycle. Users are only required to perform tasks such as schema creation and maintenance, query optimisation and security management.

The main components of *SQL Azure are* shown in Figure 2.2.

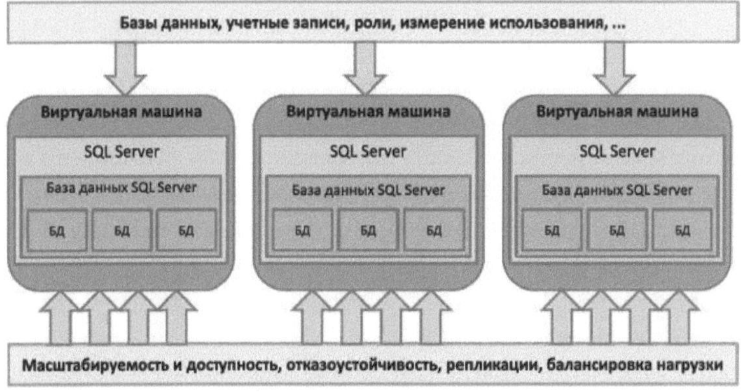

Figure 2.2. *SQL Azure* components

The Azure SQL Database instance is implemented as three replicas within the server infrastructure supported by *Cloud Fabric*. This component provides high reliability, availability and scalability through automatic and user-transparent replication and fault tolerance support. Load balancing and incremental change synchronisation across all data replicas is also supported. *Cloud Fabric* keeps track of all data change/update conflicts using bi-directional data synchronisation between replicas based on built-in or user-defined policies.

Because *SQL Azure is* built on top of *SQL Server*, users get a familiar relational data model that is nearly symmetrical with *SQL Server* servers deployed at customers' premises. Many *SQL Server* core capabilities are supported, although there are a number of limitations in the current *SQL Azure* cloud database implementation.

Four basic, high-level *SQL Azure* usage scenarios can be identified:

- Use of *SQL Azure* by applications that need to enable collaboration between users inside and outside the 'boundaries' of an organisation.

- Use of *SQL Azure* by applications hosted on *Windows Azure* infrastructure.

- Use *SQL Azure* as the foundation for building tools to consolidate data from different sources and provide26etih data to users separated geographically and working across devices.

- Using *SQL Azure in* conjunction with high load *web applications* that use relational structures to store data.

All of these scenarios address the most common challenges developers face when choosing to build applications that run on-premises, in the cloud, or hybrid applications.

Multimedia services

Windows Azure Media Services is a cloud-based *PaaS* solution that enables you to efficiently build media services and deliver media content to your customers. The solution offers a set of ready-to-use services that enable rapid media ingestion, encoding, format conversion, storage, content protection, and *live and* on-demand video delivery. *Windows Azure Media Services* also support content delivery to any device or platform, including *HTML5, Silverlight, Flash, Windows* 8, *iPad, iPhone, Android, Xbox* and *Windows Phone. In* addition, *Windows Azure Media Services* are *Microsoft Media Platform* technologies.

Windows Azure Media Services provides the following services for building your own media services and applications:

- uploading content;

- recoding;
- format conversion;
- content protection;

on demand and live streaming, as well as analytics and advertising.

This functionality is available to developers through the *REST API*, allowing them to build solutions based on *Windows Azure Media Services* using any technology that is familiar, convenient or, for example, standard in the organisation. Developers on the *.NET* platform can access the *Windows Azure Media Services SDK for .NET*, which wraps the provided *REST API* in a convenient way.

Media Services provides a range of built-in and off-the-shelf *Microsoft* and third-party components (from media sending to content distribution) that can be combined to fulfil your requirements. Capabilities available include sending, storing, encoding data, format conversion, content protection and delivery. Multimedia services can be called separately via standard *REST APIs* to facilitate integration with external applications and services.

Platform development

The platform is constantly being updated with new features. Some of the latest new features and updates, the most recent of which was in October 2018, include the following:

- support for the new platform . *NET* 4.7;
- a new management portal that came out of *Preview* state, built on *HTML5* instead of *Silverlight* (a portal that has been around since the platform's inception);
- *App Store* for additional platform components (*Addons*);
- updated *SDK* to version 1.8, which in turn brings support for *IIS8*, *C#5.0*, benefits *.NET* 4.7, *WebSockets*;
- updates for mobile services;
- updates for *web* sites;
- updates for cloud services.

One of the areas of the platform's development is the provision of mobile services that enable the creation of universal applications in the cloud that will work with mobile platforms. For example, *push notification* service, data storage in the cloud, etc. The most important feature is that *Azure*, in fact, today is more of a platform for developers and companies that build their systems in the cloud.

***Windows Azure* Store**

The *Windows Azure Marketplace* is a global online shop for *SaaS* applications and best-of-breed datasets. By submitting your *Windows Azure* apps to this site, you can sell them globally. In addition, you can subscribe your apps to a range of the best datasets on this site, or distribute your own datasets for profit.

Shop Usage Scenarios:

Gaining worldwide reach. Ability to distribute apps in many countries and accept payment in different currencies.

Unified Security Model. Enable a single security, billing, auditing and authentication model that supports single sign-on with *OAuth v2*.

Easy management of offers. Ability to use reports on traffic, subscriptions and sales.

Comparing AWS, Azure and Google Cloud

Before comparing the current market leaders of cloud providers, let's recall brief descriptions of each of them individually:

1. **Amazon Web Services** was founded in 2006 and currently provides services such as IaaS, PaaS, SaaS, etc. It also offers more than 70 resources with extended coverage in fourteen regions of the world.

2. **Azure** is a Microsoft product released in 2010. Today, the platform offers a wide range of different supporting tools, programming languages and frameworks. It runs on Microsoft Windows and Linux. About 60 services and data centres in more than 38 locations around the world are currently available on the platform. Azure customers include big names like Johnson Controls, Fujifilm, HP, Apple and some other major companies.

3. **Google Cloud Platform** is the youngest cloud platform mentioned above - it was launched in 2011 and offers a variety of services including IaaS, PaaS and Serverless, and supports Big data and IoT. The providers have over 50 resources and 6 global data centres at their disposal. To learn more about the best Google Cloud strategy for you, check out Google Cloud strategy.

AWS, Azure and Google Cloud Cloud storage

Let's compare the technologies that these leaders are using on their platforms to secure data storage.

• AWS uses Simple Storage Service (S3) for storage and Amazon's Glacier service for archiving.

• Azure and Google Cloud platforms offer storage with high performance and robust security.

• Azure is actively working on implementing and improving file backup and recovery features. The StorSimple sub-service, which is used as a hybrid storage service for enterprise customers, has significantly improved the company's efficiency. It saves up to 60 per cent of the usual cost.

AWS, Azure and Google Cloud: A Hybrid Approach

The hybrid approach is one of the latest trends that is growing quite rapidly in the world of cloud platforms.

Microsoft has long been recognised as the best option if you choose this method amongst competitors AWS, Google Cloud and Microsoft Azure, thanks to its Azure Stack software solution. The platform gives its customers the ability to host Azure cloud services on on-premises data services with open portal, code and API interfaces for easy integration and interoperability. The AWS platform showed its move towards hybrid deployment back in 2018. Later in 2019, Google executives took a step in the same direction with the release of their Anthos platform. Anthos is essentially a rebranding of Google's cloud services platform that includes Google Kubernetes Engine (GKE), GKE On-Prem, and Anthos Config Management.

AWS, Azure and Google Cloud:
Computing Power Comparison

Computing power is the backbone of any IT-related business. The main advantage of cloud platforms is that they offer efficient tools for all kinds of computing with the ability to remotely manage as well as scale regardless of time and physical location.

• AWS has a central computing network service based on Elastic Compute Cloud (EC2). It also integrates sub-services such as AWS Elastic Beanstalk, Amazon EC2 Container Service, and several other useful tools. Such tools allow enterprises to perform deep analysis and planning, minimising financial losses when starting new projects. Territorially, AWS supports regional and zonal coverage.

• Microsoft Azure uses high-performance Virtual Machine Scale Sets as a data centre. Windows client applications are deployed using RemoteApp.

• Google Cloud Platform uses the Compute Engine service for computing power. It supports most of the core cloud platform tools. The only major drawback worth mentioning is the price - it's definitely not the most flexible among the Google Cloud vs Amazon AWS vs Azure trio.

AWS and Microsoft Azure are the most popular cloud platforms in the top three. Their computing power is similar and the list of services is regularly growing. Here we would advise you to read more about ensuring cloud scalability.

Comparing AWS, Azure and Google Cloud: Analysis

All platforms provide access to some effective analytics tools.

• AWS has made a breakthrough by launching the Quick Sight analytics service. It includes ready-made templates, and the service itself is cheaper compared to classic BI solutions.

• Microsoft Azure has improved its analytics and machine learning tools, as well as created a Data Lake Analytics subsystem and introduced machine learning.

• A special area of Big Data analytics is now available in Google Cloud. Cloud Vision API, Cloud Speech API and Google Translate API projects can be integrated into third-party resources.

Network load balancing

Load balancing services are available in GCP and Azure. They distribute traffic to improve fault tolerance:

1. HTTP load balance (S)

Layer 7 load balancing is available in Azure and Google, meaning that client requests at the application layer can tolerate more complex routing than the previous layer 4c.

2. TCP / UDP load balance

Among Google Cloud, Amazon Web Services, and Microsoft Azure platforms, Layer 4 balancing is available with Azure and Google platforms. They evenly distribute client requests across the region via network routes.

3. SSL load balance

The same two providers, Azure and Google, also support SSL.

AWS, Azure and Google Cloud: Security

Microsoft and Google are known for their high level of security when it comes to cloud storage. Both vendors have built a model based on more than a decade of development history.

This high level of security is provided in three ways:

1. The security of the cloud platform itself is achieved through the cloud platform's inbuilt infrastructure, which provides default protection.

2. Security in a cloud-based platform with access to security products and services that can be customised to protect personal applications and data.

3. Security Anywhere - Advanced security capabilities beyond the cloud platform to protect user assets regardless of location.

In addition, Google and Azure enforce their security policies in compliance with CSA STAR, GDPR, HIPPA, PCI-DSS and ISO standards.

The level of security Azure has today is the highest among the three cloud platforms in our survey. It meets more than 90 quality criteria in 50 regions around the world. For reference, only 45 of the available options meet Google's requirements.

AWS, Azure and Google Cloud: cost

The three cloud platforms have different approaches to pricing when using the services.

AWS offers three payment options:

Option 1: You simply pay for the resources you use.

Option 2. Try the resources and services you are going to order. Users are given 1 to 3 years upfront, after which services are paid for based on usage. Discounts of up to 75% off the regular price are available from time to time.

Option 3. The more you use the services, the less you pay.

Amazon Web Services fees are calculated based on each hour of usage.

Microsoft Azure offers a different pricing scheme. Vendor resources are paid with rounding up for each minute. Discounts are provided depending on the volume of services used.

GCP works on the same principles as Azure, but with the exception that the total cost is rounded up every 10 minutes of usage.

Platforms have created special calculation services to analyse commissions to make it easier.

AWS, Azure and Google Cloud: Advantages and Disadvantages

• *Access Zones: with* more regions and access zones, AWS has a distinct advantage.

• *Market Share:* Amazon Web Services covers approximately one-third of the total market share.

• *Number of services:* AWS is the leader.

• *Integration with open source and on-premises systems (MS tools)*: Azure is one of the most versatile platforms.

• *Billing models*: flexible pricing model and frequent discounts make Google Cloud the most affordable platform.

While AWS leads in many aspects when comparing google cloud, azure and AWS, Azure and Google Cloud are not lagging behind either:

AWS Strengths	AWS Weaknesses
✔ Most mature, enterprise-ready provider	✘ Requires advanced technical expertise to implement
✔ Broad collection of services and partner ecosystem	✘ Lacks strong hybrid cloud support
✔ Recommended for all use cases that run well in a virtualized environment	✘ Extensive catalogue of offerings can be overwhelming to navigate

Azure Strengths

✓ Seamless integrations with other Microsoft products and services

✓ Improved support for Linux and open-source applications stacks

✓ Ideal for hybrid cloud

✓ Recommended for all use cases that run well in a virtualized environment

Azure Weaknesses

✗ Poor support for large-scale implementations

✗ Advanced technical expertise is required to implement Azure in a reliable, secure way

✗ Historical issues with infrastructure reliability

Google Cloud Strengths

✓ Great reputation in the open-source community

✓ Deep investments in analytics and machine learning

✓ Recommended for big data and analytics applications, ML projects and cloud-native applications

Google Cloud Weaknesses

✗ Rigid in contract negotiations

✗ Small partner ecosystem

✗ Limited range of services for larger companies

Comparison of AWS, Azure and Google Cloud services

AWS: Positive and Negative Aspects

AWS was ahead of its competitors by building a suite of cloud services back in 2006. AWS offers a wide and regularly growing range of offerings, as well as the widest network of global data centres among others. The provider is constantly improving the security and reliability of the platform. AWS's partner ecosystem and overall product strategy is considered a market leader, with the AWS Marketplace offering a wide range of third-party software services. As Gartner notes in its <u>Magic Quadrant for Cloud Infrastructure as a Service, Worldwide</u>:

"AWS has been the market leader in cloud IaaS for over 10 years"

One of the disadvantages of AWS is the large selection of what the platform offers. While having a large number of resources is more of an advantage, it can be difficult for users to navigate the many features available.

In addition, the top three are Google Cloud, Amazon Cloud or Azure AWS - Azure AWS is the most expensive solution. Despite the fact that the platform regularly lowers prices and offers discounts, it is sometimes difficult for companies to calculate costs and effectively manage expenses when using a large number of different tool resources.

Microsoft Azure: Positive and Negative Aspects

A significant advantage of Azure is that the platform communicates effectively with Microsoft's core on-premises systems (Windows Server, System Center and Active Directory).

According to a January 2020 Goldman Sachs survey of 100 IT executives, 56 of them said they prefer Azure to Amazon Web Services' cloud platform.

Microsoft is also increasingly embracing open source technology. Today, at least half of the company's workloads run on Linux.

One of the downsides of this cloud service is a series of outages, including a major resource outage in May 2019. If we analyse the history of Google Cloud, AWS or Azure, AWS is also not immune to outages, but its last major outage occurred. in 2017, when cloud technology was a bit younger, and in the Google Cloud service the last major outage occurred in November 2019.

Many organisations are also unhappy with the quality of Microsoft's technical support, so this is something to consider when choosing a platform.

Azure ARM Templates

With the move to cloud platforms, management practices have also changed to be more flexible and adaptable. Teams now manage infrastructure and application code through a single, automated deployment process. To do this, Azure uses ARM templates or JSON files. Azure templates allow you to create and deploy platform infrastructure: networking, virtual machines, storage, etc.

Deploy infrastructure repeatedly throughout the development cycle with Azure. Azure Resource Manager templates allow you to deploy templates multiple times with a consistent project state. This way, you don't have to create them separately for each individual update. Resource Manager also runs a series of Azure deployment templates simultaneously with a single command.

GCP: Positive and Negative Aspects

Google developed the Kubernetes standard, which was later implemented by Amazon Web Services and Microsoft Azure. GCP specialises in high computing power, offering Big data, analytics and machine learning.

However, users are not satisfied with errors in processes related to corporate accounts. Sometimes it hampers the ability to conduct transactions. Some of the shortcomings are evident in areas such as contract negotiation, independent software vendor (ISV) licensing, integration with enterprise systems, and customer support.

It is also important to note that Google has the lowest presence among Google Cloud Platforms compared to AWS and Azure, and it is absent in one of the world's largest markets - China. In contrast, AWS and Azure have a presence in mainland China - Beijing Sinnet Technology, NWDC and 21Vianet.

Comparing AWS, Azure and Google Cloud: properties

Choosing a cloud provider depends on the needs and workloads of your business - medium or large. The table below lists the services of cloud computing leaders.

External applications can be run on all three platforms. For example, Google has partnerships with SAP, Pivotal and Rackspace.

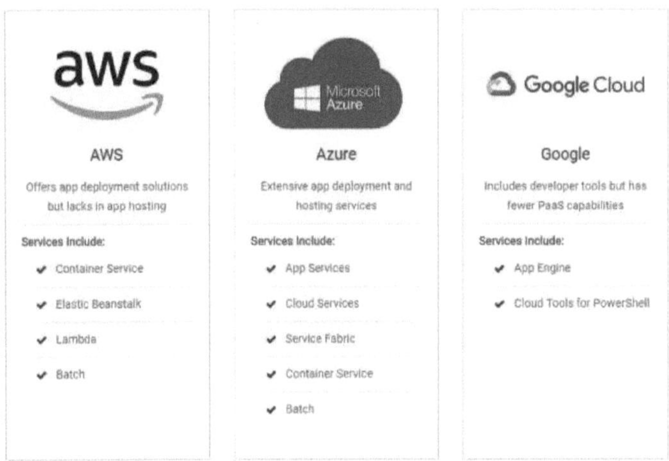

AWS, Azure and GCP: Key Differences

The table below has a list of the key differences between the leaders in cloud solutions.

AWS vs Azure vs Google Cloud comparison chart:

Vendor	Strengths	Weaknesses
AWS	• Dominant market position • Extensive, mature offerings • Support for large organisations • Extensive training • Global reach	• Difficult to use • Cost management • Overwhelming options
Microsoft Azure	-Second largest provider • Integration with Microsoft tools and software • Broad feature set • Hybrid cloud • Support for open source	-Issues with documentation - Incomplete management tooling
Google	• Designed for cloud native businesses • Commitment to open source and portability • Deep discounts and flexible contracts • DevOps expertise	• Late entrant to IaaS market • Fewer features and services • Historically not as enterprise focused

Conclusions

Whether to use or ignore cloud providers is no longer a question for business owners and developers. The big question today is which platform to choose

Google Cloud vs Amazon Web Services vs Microsoft Azure. Which cloud platform is right for you? Newbies can make their choice based on the cost factor of platform resources. But there are other features that are important to consider when deciding which is the best platform: Google Cloud, Microsoft Azure or AWS.

When choosing the right cloud provider, it's worth considering your specific needs and your company's workload. After exploring and comparing their features in our article, we suggest you try a free trial of each and choose the platform that best suits your needs.

Threat and security issues for cloud computing

With cloud computing, the main issue that concerns users is related to their security. One issue is that cloud providers themselves may have access to unencrypted customer data - whether it is on disc, in memory or transmitted over the network.

Security threats to cloud computing

Threats relate to potential damage to resources, such as information, processes and systems, and therefore to organisations. Threats can be of natural or man-made origin and can be accidental or intentional. Threats can occur within or outside the organisation. Threats can be categorised as accidental or intentional, and active or passive.

The specific threats detected are highly dependent on the specific cloud service chosen. For example, with respect to public cloud, threats may arise from the division of responsibilities between Cloud Service Customer (CSC) and Cloud Service Provider (*CSP*): Difficulties in defining jurisdiction over data and processes, consistency and adequacy of data protection, privacy assurance, etc. However, in a private cloud it is easier to address threats because the CSC has control over all tenants hosted by the CSP.

Security threats to cloud service consumers (CSC)

The following threats directly affect CSC. They may affect a CSC's personal or business interests, privacy, legitimacy or security. Not all CSCs are at risk from all threats. The risk is not uniform and depends on the nature of the CSC and the cloud computing service used.

Data loss and leakage. Due to the fact that there are usually multiple tenants in a cloud service environment, data loss or leakage is a serious threat to CSC. Lack of proper management of cryptographic information such as encryption keys, authentication codes and access rights can cause serious damage such as data loss or unexpected leakage outside the cloud. The main sources of this threat can be considered to be, for   example,   insufficient management tools

authentication, authorisation and auditing, inconsistent use of encryption and/or authentication keys, operational failures

Unprotected access to the service. Identity credentials, including CSC administrator credentials, are particularly vulnerable to unauthorised users in a highly distributed cloud computing environment. The reason is that, unlike in traditional telecommunications, it is often difficult to use the location (e.g., fixed-line telephone) or the presence of a specific piece of hardware (e.g., mobile subscriber identity module (SIM)) to prove identity authentication.

Because most of the services offered are remote, unsecured connections are potentially vulnerable.

Internal threats. Where an individual is involved, there is always a risk that the actions of individuals will prove incompatible with the security of the service. CSC staff sharing administrator passwords or otherwise leaving login details unsecured (e.g. written on a piece of paper taped to the screen), careless or inadequately trained users (or family members in the consumer's immediate environment) or malicious actions of disgruntled staff are always a threat.

Security Threats to Cloud Service Providers (CSPs)

These threats directly affect the CSP. Such threats may affect a CSP's ability to offer services, conduct operations, retain customers, and avoid legal or regulatory difficulties.

Unauthorised administrative access. A cloud computing service includes interfaces and software components that allow the CSC's own personnel to perform administrative functions with respect to aspects of the cloud computing service that are under the control of the CSC, such as adding or removing CSC employee accounts, connecting to the CSC's own servers, changing bandwidth, updating Domain Name System (DNS) and website records, and so forth. Such administrative interfaces can be targeted by attackers who impersonate CSC administrators to attack CSPs.

Internal threats. Where human involvement is involved, there is always a risk that malicious or careless actions by individuals will jeopardise the security of the service. CSC staff sharing administrator passwords or otherwise leaving login details unsecured (e.g. written on a piece of paper taped to the screen), careless or inadequately trained users or malicious actions by disgruntled staff always pose a serious threat to any activity.

Cloud computing security issues

Security issues include difficulties other than the immediate security threat, including "indirect" threats, which are due to the nature and operating environment of cloud services. An indirect threat occurs when a threat to one user of a cloud service can have negative consequences for other users.

Security concerns for cloud service consumers (CSC)

Uncertainty of responsibility. The consumption of provided resources is carried out by CSCs under different service categories and deployment models. Thus, the ICT system created by the customer depends on these services. Any lack of clearly defined responsibilities between the CSC and the CSP may cause conflicts of principle or operational conflicts. Any inconsistency in the provisions of the service contract may provoke irregularities or incidents. For example, at the international level, it may be a problem that there is no clear distinction between which entity is the controller of personal data and which is the processor of personal data, even if the international dimension is limited to a small third-party organisation outside a particular region, such as the European Union.

Any ambiguity related to legal and regulatory requirements (e.g., whether a CSC or CSP is a "personal data controller" or a "personal data processor") may lead to uncertainty as to which set of regulations it is required to comply with. If this interpretation varies from jurisdiction to jurisdiction, a given CSC or CSP may be subject to conflicting regulations relating to the same service or piece of data.

Loss of trust. In some cases, it is difficult for a CSC to recognise the trust level of its CSP due to the black box nature of the cloud computing service. In the absence of a means of obtaining information about the trust level of the provider and sharing this information in a formalised way, the CSC has no means of assessing the level of security implementation achieved by the provider. This lack of sharing of security level information regarding CSPs may pose a serious security risk to some CSCs in their use of cloud computing services.

Loss of control. A CSC's decision to migrate part of their own ICT system to a cloud computing infrastructure implies a transfer of partial control to the CSP. Such a move could be a serious threat to CSC data, especially in relation to the role and privileges assigned to the provider. Combined with a lack of transparency about the cloud provider's practices, this could lead to misconfiguration or even provide the opportunity for a malicious insider attack.

When adopting cloud computing services, some CSCs may have concerns about the lack of control over their own information and resources hosted by CSPs with respect to data storage, reliability of data backup (data retention issues), countermeasures in business continuity plans (BCPs), disaster recovery, etc.

For example:

- The CSC wants to delete the file for legal reasons, but the CSP retains a copy that the CSC is unaware of.

- The CSP grants CSC administrator privileges that are outside the scope of the CSC policy.

- Some CSCs may have concerns about CSPs disclosing data to foreign governments, which may affect CSCs' compliance with privacy laws, such as European Union data protection directives.

Loss of Privacy. When CSPs process sensitive information, there is the potential for a privacy breach, which may also include a breach of applicable regulations, certifications or data protection laws. This includes leaking sensitive information or processing personally identifiable information (PII) for purposes that are not authorised by CSC and/or the data subject.

Service unreadiness. Readiness is not exclusively related to the cloud computing environment. However, due to the principle of service-oriented design, service delivery may be affected if higher-level cloud computing services are not fully ready. In addition, the dynamic dependency of cloud computing provides more opportunities for attackers. For example, in the same cloud computing system, a denial-of-service attack on one upstream service may affect several downstream services.

Binding to a single cloud service provider. High dependency on a single CSP can make it difficult to replace one CSP with another. This can occur when a CSP uses non-standard features or formats and does not provide interoperability. If the CSP to which the "tethering" is performed does not address a known security vulnerability, a security risk may arise and thus the CSC is vulnerable but has no way of migrating to another CSP.

Loss of software integrity. Since the CSC software runs in the CSP, there is the possibility of the software being altered or infected by a virus when it leaves the direct control of the CSC. Thus, this causes the CSC software to malfunction, manifesting itself in one way or another. Whilst CSC is unable to control this possibility, it could seriously affect its reputation and therefore its operations.

Security challenges for cloud service providers (CSPs)

Uncertainty about responsibilities. Different roles (CSP, CSC and CSN) may be defined in a cloud computing system. Uncertainty regarding the definition of responsibilities related to issues such as data ownership, access control or infrastructure maintenance may affect business or legal disputes (especially when interacting with third parties, or if the CSP is also a CSC or CSN). This risk of uncertainty is increased if the CSP operates and/or offers services in multiple jurisdictions where contracts and agreements may exist in different languages or be based on different legal and regulatory frameworks.

Shared environment. Cloud computing offers potential savings by sharing large amounts of resources on an extremely large scale. In this situation, many potentially vulnerable interfaces are unprotected. For example, different CSCs simultaneously use services from the same cloud. As a result, a CSC could theoretically gain unauthorised access to virtual machines, network traffic, real/residual data and other resources of other tenants. Any such unauthorised or malicious access to another CSC's resources may compromise their integrity, availability and confidentiality.

Inconsistency and conflict of protection mechanisms. Due to the decentralised architecture of cloud computing infrastructure, its security mechanisms may be inconsistent across different distributed security modules. For example, access denied by one security module may be granted by another module. Such inconsistency may create problems for an authorised user and it can be exploited by an attacker, and thus lead to violation of confidentiality, integrity and availability.

Failed migration and integration. Moving to the cloud often involves moving large amounts of data and major configuration changes (e.g., network addressing). Moving one part of the ICT system to be serviced by an external CSP may require significant system design (e.g., network and security policies). Failed integration caused by incompatible interfaces or inconsistent policy enforcement can lead to both functional and non-functional consequences. For example, virtual machines that in a private data centre operate under firewall protection in a CSP cloud are susceptible to open internet incidents.

Business interruptions. In cloud computing, resources are allocated and delivered as a service. The entire cloud computing ecosystem consists of many interdependent parts. An outage in any part (e.g., power outage, denial of service, or delay) can affect the availability of the cloud computing service, and further lead to business interruptions.

Supply Chain Vulnerability. A CSP is at risk if hardware or software provided to the platform through its supply chain compromises the security of the CSC or CSP, for example by accidentally or deliberately introducing malware or vulnerabilities that can be exploited.

An example is defective CSN software. This security issue concerns CSN software running on CSP hardware, such as client software, virtual machine (VM), guest operating system (OS), applications, platform components, or auditing/monitoring software (e.g., for a partner providing service auditing).

LITERATURE

1. Kononyuk A.E. Fundamental theory of cloud technologies. - In 18 books. Book 1. -K.: Osvgga Ukrashi. 2018.- 620 c.

2. Stefanovsky I.L. Introduction to cloud computing: manual / Ministry of Education of the Republic of Belarus, Gomel State Technical University named after P.O. Sukhoi. P.O. Sukhoi. - Gomel: P.O. Sukhoi State Technical University, 2019. - 113 c.

3. *George Reese. Cloud Application Architectures.* 2009. - 208 p. (George Reese. Cloud Computing: Per. from Engl. - SPb.: BHV-Peterburg, 2011. - 288 c.)

4. Badenko V.L. High-performance computing: textbook - St. Petersburg: Izd-vo Polytechnicheskiye un-ta, 2010. - 180 c.

5. Sergey Platonov. File systems: from discs to clouds. Storage News No. 2 (54), 2013.

6. https://seti.ucoz.ru/index/prodolzhenie lekcii 18/0-142

7. https: //intuit. ru/studies/courses/12226/1178/lecture/19676

8. Amazon Web Services Overview. https://d1.awsstatic.com/whitepapers/ru RU/aws-overview.pdf

Printed by Books on Demand GmbH, Norderstedt / Germany